THE SIREN
AND SELECTED WRITINGS

Giuseppe Tomasi (1896–1957), Prince of Lampedusa and an indigent survivor of the great Sicilian landed aristocracy, is best remembered as the author of *The Leopard*, considered by L. P. Hartley to be "perhaps the greatest novel of the century". Being a man of broad culture, his acquaintance with Italian and foreign literatures was remarkably deep and perceptive, and not least his love and understanding of English literature, down to the minor luminaries seldom read outside the literature faculties. Stendhal was of all French writers his favourite, as is clear from the warmth of his writing in the present volume. A man who cultivated the extempore and the conversational, he died having published nothing, but leaving the basis for his vast posthumous reputation.

David Gilmour is author of *The Last Leopard: A Life of Giuseppe Tomasi di Lampedusa* (published in Harvill paperback) and, among other books, of a biography of Lord Curzon which was awarded the Duff Cooper prize.

By the same author

THE LEOPARD

Giuseppe Tomasi di Lampedusa

THE SIREN AND SELECTED WRITINGS

*Translated from the Italian
by Archibald Colquhoun, David Gilmour
and Guido Waldman*

with Introductions by David Gilmour

THE HARVILL PRESS
LONDON

Places of my Infancy   *The Professor and the Siren*   *The Blind Kittens*
(all translated by Archibald Colquhoun)
First published in Italian with the title *Racconti* by Giangiacomo Feltrinelli Editore,
Milan, 1961
First published in Great Britain by Collins and Harvill, 1962
© Giangiacomo Feltrinelli Editore 1961
English translation © William Collins Sons & Co Ltd and Pantheon Books 1961, 1962

Joy and the Law   (translated by Guido Waldman)
First published in Italian in the collection *Racconti* by Giangiacomo Feltrinelli Editore,
Milan, 1961
This translation first published in Great Britain in the anthology *Leopard II: Turning
the Page*, by Harvill, 1993
© Giangiacomo Feltrinelli Editore 1961 English translation © HarperCollins 1993

English Literature   (translated by David Gilmour)
First published in Italian with the title *Letteratura inglese* by Arnoldo Mondadori,
Milan, 1990, 1991
This selection first published in Great Britain by The Harvill Press, 1995
© Arnoldo Mondadori 1990, 1991 English translation © The Harvill Press 1995

Tutorials on Stendhal   (translated by David Gilmour)
First published in Italian with the title *Lezioni su Stendhal* by Sellerio Editore, Palermo,
1977
This selection first published in Great Britain by The Harvill Press, 1995
© Sellerio Editore 1977 English translation © The Harvill Press 1995

This edition © The Harvill Press 1995
Second impression

The Harvill Press
84 Thornhill Road
London N1 1RD

A CIP catalogue record for this book
is available from the British Library.

ISBN 1 86046 021 6 hardback
1 86046 022 4 paperback

Set in Monophoto Bembo
by Servis Filmsetting Limited, Manchester

Printed and bound in Great Britain by
Hartnolls Ltd., Bodmin, Cornwall

Contents

ENGLISH LITERATURE

Introduction to the Memory
and Three Stories,

BY DAVID GILMOUR

Giuseppe Tomasi, Prince of Lampedusa, compressed almost his entire creative work into the last two and a half years of his life. Before reaching the age of fifty-eight he had written nothing beyond three essays for an obscure Genoese journal in the 1920s. Yet thirty months before his death in 1957 he finally accepted his literary vocation and embarked on a short and vigorous career that overcame advancing ill-health to produce several drafts of one novel, the opening chapter of a second, a childhood memoir and two short stories. None of these were published in his lifetime, but two years after his death his great novel *The Leopard* won the Strega Prize and within twenty years had sold over a million copies, gone through 121 editions and been translated into twenty-three languages. An unknown Sicilian nobleman has posthumously become Italy's literary sensation of the century.

Lampedusa had been planning to write fiction for at least twenty years before he settled down to do so. The last, childless and impoverished member of a family that liked to trace its ancestry back to the Byzantine Empire, he felt the need to record something of that long decadence which concluded in the destruction of the Palazzo Lampedusa in Palermo during the Second World War. He wanted also to evoke the Sicily of his childhood, the twilight years of the old aristocracy during the Belle Epoque, before its fading traces disappeared. Yet laziness and that peculiar Sicilian diffidence, which he shared with his cousin, the poet Lucio Piccolo, held him back. Only after Piccolo eventually published his poems – and won a prize for them in 1954 – did Lampedusa feel sufficient confidence to compete in the literary arena. "Being mathematically certain," he told a friend, "that I was no more of a fool [than Lucio], I sat down at my desk and wrote a novel."

After spending the early months of 1955 writing and rewriting the long first chapter, Lampedusa interrupted the novel in order to write his autobiography. His widow later stated that she had encouraged him to do so to mitigate the desolation suffered from the loss of his family homes and to "neutralise his nostalgia". But the composition of his memoirs also helped his fictional writing: the evocation of his mother's family home at Santa Margherita certainly made it easier for him to visualise the great palace at Donnafugata. Another stimulus was provided by re-reading Stendhal's autobiography, *Vie de Henri Brulard*, written in a style which he attempted to emulate.

Lampedusa intended to cover his entire life. But after completing only the chapters on his childhood, which deal largely with Santa Margherita and the Palazzo Lampedusa, he abandoned the project and returned to the novel. He never revised the chapters, and after his death his widow edited the manuscript and published it together with the short stories.

A Freudian psychoanalyst, half-Italian and half-German Balt, Alessandra di Lampedusa survived her husband for a quarter of a century and made herself a tenacious custodian of his reputation. While she may have been right in some cases to deter aspiring biographers, her mutilation of Lampedusa's memoirs was in several respects unfortunate. To impose some topographical coherence on her husband's rather random recollections, she altered the sequences of numerous passages. While this rearrangement makes the text easier to follow – and has therefore generally been adopted in this edition – it occasionally distorts the meaning entirely. In the princess's version, for example, Lampedusa's dog is alleged to have looked reproachfully at his young master after he had shot two robins, but the original text states that the reproach was communicated when he stroked the dog after crushing the evil-smelling berries of a castor-oil shrub.

Other changes originated from a misreading of her husband's handwriting, a misunderstanding of certain words and, more frequently, a misplaced sense of propriety. References to scandals involving Lampedusa's ancestors – even if long since dead – were excised, as was a remark about the masculinity of one of his female cousins. Other exclusions seem incomprehensible. One blameless individual who played Chopin nocturnes in the evening was struck out, and the princess's obsession with the anonymity of dead, unlibelled characters made her change even the names of places they visited, in one case ruining a story by substituting Viterbo for Frascati. The missing figures were included in a new Italian edition in 1988 and appear here for the first time in English.

Lampedusa worked on *The Leopard* for the rest of 1955 and for most of the following year. The first few months of 1957, before learning he had lung cancer in May, were the most productive of his life. Apart from adding two chapters and writing a further draft of the whole novel, he composed the three fictional pieces in this volume.

In December 1956 the Lampedusas were sent a panettone for Christmas. Its arrival stimulated the prince to begin "Joy and the Law", a story unlike anything else he wrote which – perhaps for that reason – was omitted from previous English editions of his minor writings. It is a compassionate tale about a poor clerk and his family in Palermo, a short and unambitious story which nevertheless manages to evoke the corrosive tentacles of Sicilian life and the absurd code of honour under which people are forced to live. Although there is no reference to the Mafia or hint of violence, more pacific aspects of Sicilian corruption – patronage and exploitation – are handled with skill. So are the humiliations of the protagonist, the saintly and inflexible character of his wife, and the tattered decay of post-war Palermo.

"Joy and the Law" was followed by "The Siren", a fable about death and mortality which spans the classical Mediterranean and the twentieth century. One does not need to read the crop of psychoanalytical studies of the tale to appreciate the beauty of its language or the vastness of its themes. Just as *The Leopard* evoked the "archaic and aromatic countryside" of inland Sicily, so "The Siren" contains incomparable descriptions of the sea and the coastline, "the enchantment of certain summer nights within sight of Castellamare Bay, when stars are mirrored in the sleeping sea and the spirit of anyone lying back amid the lentisks is lost in a vortex of sky, while the body is tense and alert, fearing the approach of demons".

The author put much of himself into the story. Like the narrator, Paolo Corbera, he had been in Augusta as a recruit and in Turin as a young man. Like Corbera too, he was the last member of an aristocratic family whose home had been destroyed by "Liberators" in the Second World War. But there is even more of Lampedusa in Rosario La Ciura, the dogmatic and irritable old Hellenist who shares some of his creator's enthusiasms (such as Shakespeare), his dislikes (such as academics, melodrama and H. G. Wells) and his exasperation with the "donkeys" who inhabit Sicily: "I imagine nothing good ever happens there, as it hasn't for three thousand years."

The Leopard has themes that are grand enough, the decay of a noble family, the destruction of its society and the corruption of the Risorgimento ideals. But "The Siren" expands them to encompass the ruin of the Mediterranean and the classical world over the subsequent millennia. The fatalism and anger shared by Lampedusa and La Ciura stem from their vision of their island's history, from their view of human "progress" there since the days of the early Greek colonists. Critics who lambasted their idea of the Sicilian past failed to see that the writer, like many of his fellow islanders who live in their birthplace, loved Sicily as much as he hated it, and that the hatred was a direct consequence and in direct proportion to the extent of its decadence. His island, whose fertility had enticed droves of classical immigrants, had become the shame of southern Europe, its violence and aridity forcing millions of its people to emigrate. Like La Ciura, Lampedusa held the view that no place had so much natural beauty as Sicily and no place had been so corrupted by its people and its rulers.

The last of his shorter works is the opening chapter of a novel he planned to call *I gattini ciechi* ("The Blind Kittens"). The author intended to trace the rise and fall of the Ibbas, a peasant family of prototype *mafiosi* who had made their money through "an epic of cunning and perfidy, of ruthlessness and defiance of the law", and were destined to lose much of their greedily accumulated estates through land reform after the Second World War. As a counterpoint, Lampedusa introduces a group of fatuous noblemen discussing the Ibbas' rise in the aristocratic club of Palermo. Although they belong to his own class, the author finds them scarcely more attractive than the family they are talking about. People with "frothy and infantile imaginations" and a "low consumption of general ideas", they provide a pitiful spectacle, "the tragic jerking of a class" a few minutes from oblivion. Perhaps their most useful literary role is to refute the theory that Lampedusa was a reactionary writer.

Although it is difficult to judge the quality of a novel from the first chapter, it seems unlikely that *I gattini ciechi* would have been in the same class as *The Leopard*. Compared to both that novel and "The Siren", its theme is a meagre one. There is no character, moreover, whom Lampedusa could identify with, no protagonist of the intelligence or sensibility of La Ciura or *The Leopard*'s Don Fabrizio. Wholly devoid of human sympathy, the first chapter reads like the overture to a novel in which the Ibbas and the noblemen would merely compete as targets for the author's unceasing sarcasm.

The irritable and almost cantankerous style can at least partly be attributed to Lampedusa's increasing ill-health. During that fertile spring he had bronchitis and emphysema and suspected he might have tuberculosis. After it was diagnosed that in fact he had cancer, his morale collapsed. Nevertheless, he was persuaded to go to Rome in May for a course of cobalt treatment. Transformed by now from a dilettante to a writer with a mission, he worked on his manuscripts in a clinic while his wife and sister-in-law typed them out under his direction. Shortly before his death in July, he received the news that *The Leopard* had been rejected for a second time by a leading publisher. Disheartened though he was, he left instructions to his adopted son that the novel should not be published at his expense. He knew its worth and would not countenance the humiliation of having to pay for its publication. Yet even he would have been surprised by the scale of his posthumous vindication.

PLACES OF MY INFANCY

I

With everyone, I think, memories of early childhood consist of a series of visual impressions, many very clear but lacking any sense of chronology. To write a "chronicle" of one's own childhood is, it seems, impossible; however honest one might set out to be one would eventually give a false impression, often with glaring anachronisms. I shall therefore adopt the method of grouping my subjects together, so trying to give an overall impression in space rather than by sequence of time. I will touch on the background of my childhood and of the people forming part of it; also of my feelings, though I will not try to follow the development of these from their origins.

I can promise to say nothing that is untrue, but I shall not want to say *all*; and I reserve the right to lie by omission. Unless I change my mind.

One of the oldest memories I can set exactly in time, as it is connected with a fact verifiable historically, goes back to the 30th of July 1900, and so to the time when I was a few days over three and a half years old.

I was with my mother in her dressing-room, with her maid (probably Teresa from Turin). It was a rectangular room whose windows gave on to a pair of balconies projecting from the shorter sides, one of them looking over a narrow garden that separated our house from the Oratory of S. Zita, the other over a small inner courtyard. The dressing-table, kidney-shaped, with a pink material showing through its glass top and legs enwrapped in a kind of white lace petticoat, was set facing the balcony overlooking the little garden; on it, as well as brushes and toilet implements, stood a big mirror in a frame also made of mirror, decorated with stars and other glass ornaments which were a delight to me.

It was about eleven in the morning, I think, and I can see the great light of summer coming through the open French windows, whose shutters were closed.

My mother was combing her hair with the help of her maid, and I do not know what I could have been doing, sitting on the floor in the middle of the room. I don't know if my nurse, Elvira the Sienese, was with us too, but I think not.

Suddenly we hear hurried steps coming up the little inner staircase communicating with my father's apartments on the lower or *mezzanine* floor directly beneath; he enters without knocking, and utters some phrase in an excited tone. I remember his manner very well, but not his words nor their sense.

I can "see" still, though, the effect they produced; my mother dropped the long-handled silver brush she was holding, Teresa said; "*Bon Signour!*", and the whole room was in consternation.

My father had come to announce the assassination of King Umberto at Monza the evening before, the 29th of July 1900. I repeat that I "see" every streak of light and shade from the balcony, "hear" my father's excited voice, the sound of the brush falling on the glass table top, good Teresa's exclamation in Piedmontese, that I "feel" the sense of dismay which over-whelmed us; but all this remains personal, detached from the news of the King's death. The historic meaning, as it were, was told me later, and may serve to explain the persistence of the scene in my memory.

Another of the memories which I can clearly distinguish is that of the Messina earthquake (28th December 1908). The shock was certainly felt at Palermo, but I have no memory of that; I suppose it did not interrupt my sleep. But I can see distinctly the hands of my grandfather's big English pendulum-clock, which was then incongruously located in the big winter drawing-room, stopped at the fatal hour of twenty past five; and I can still hear one of my uncles (I think Ferdinando who was mad about watchmaking) explain to me that it had been stopped by an earthquake during the night. Then I remember that same evening, about half past seven, being in my grandparents' dining-room (I used often to be present at their dinner as it took place before mine) when an uncle, probably the same Ferdinando, came in with an evening paper which announced "serious damage and numerous victims at Messina from this morning's earthquake".

I speak of "my grandparents' dining-room", but I should say my grandmother's, because my grandfather had been dead a year and a month.

This memory is much less lively visually than the first, though much more exact on the other hand from the point of view of a "thing that happened".

Some days later there arrived from Messina my cousin Filippo who had lost his father and mother in the earthquake. He went to stay with my cousins the Piccolos, together with his cousin Adamo, and I remember going there to pay him a visit on a bleak rainy winter's day. I remember that he had a camera (already!) which he had taken care to keep with him as he escaped from the ruins of his house in Via della Rovere, and how on a table by a window he drew the outlines of warships and discussed with Casimiro the calibre of the guns and the emplacement of the turrets; his insouciant attitude amid the dreadful misadventures he had undergone was criticised at the time by his family, though it was charitably ascribed to shock resulting from the disaster – this was said to be prevalent among all the survivors of Messina. It was later more accurately put down to a cold nature which only caught fire in addressing technical questions such as, precisely, photography and the turrets on the early dreadnoughts.

I can still see my mother's grief when, quite a few days later, came news of her sister Lina's and her brother-in-law's bodies having been found. I can see my mother, dressed in a short cape of moiré Astrakhan, sobbing in a big armchair in the green drawing-room, an armchair in which no one ever sat, though it's the very one in which I "see" my great-grandmother sitting. Big army wagons were going round the streets collecting clothes and blankets for refugees; one passed along Via di Lampedusa and I handed woollen blankets from one of our balconies over to a soldier standing up on a cart and almost level with the balcony. This soldier was an artilleryman, with orange braid on his blue forage cap; I can still see his rubicund face and hear his "Thank you, m'boy," in a mainland accent. I have a memory, too, of a rumour going round that the refugees, who were lodged everywhere, even in boxes at theatres, were behaving " most indecently" among themselves, and of my father saying with a smile, "They feel an urge to replace the dead," an allusion which I understood perfectly.

I retain no clear recollection of my Aunt Lina, who died in the earthquake; (her demise opened the sequence of tragic deaths among my mother's sisters, which provides a sampling of the three kinds of death by violence – accident, murder and suicide). She seldom came to Palermo: I do remember her husband, though, with his lively pair of eyes behind his glasses, and an unkempt, grizzled little beard.

There is another day also clearly stamped on my memory; I cannot get the date exactly, but it was certainly a long time before the Messina earthquake and shortly after King Umberto's death, I think. We were guests of the Florios at their villa of Favignana, at the height of summer. I remember Erica, my nurse, coming to wake me up earlier than usual, about seven, hurriedly passing a sponge full of cold water over my face and then dressing me with great care. I was dragged downstairs, went out through a little side-door to the garden, then made to climb up on to the villa's main entrance veranda overlooking the sea, and reached by a flight of some six or seven steps. I remember the blinding sun of that early morning of July or August. On the veranda, which was protected from the sun by great curtains of orange cloth swelling and flapping like sails in the sea breeze (I can still hear the sound), my mother, Signora Florio (the "divinely lovely" Franca) and others were sitting on cane-chairs. In the centre of the group sat a very old, very bent lady with an aquiline nose, enwrapped in widow's weeds which were waving wildly about in the wind. I was brought before her; she said a few words which I did not understand and, bending down even farther, gave me a kiss on the forehead. (I must have been very small indeed if a lady sitting down had to bend down even farther to kiss me.) After this I was taken back to my room, stripped of my finery, redressed in more modest garments and led on to the beach to join the Florio children and others: with them I bathed and we stayed for a long time under a broiling sun playing our favourite game, which was searching in the sand for pieces of deep red coral occasionally to be found there.

That afternoon it was revealed that the old lady had been Eugénie, ex-Empress of the French, whose yacht was anchored off Favignana; she had dined with the Florios the night before (without of course my knowing anything about it) and had paid a farewell visit at seven next morning, (thus with imperial nonchalance inflicting real torture on my mother and on Signora Florio), in the course of which her hosts had wished to present to her the younger members of the household. It appears that the words she uttered before kissing me were: *"Quel joli petit!"*

During these last few days (mid-June, 1955) I have been rereading Stendhal's *Henri Brulard*. I had not read it since long ago in 1922, when I must have still been obsessed by "explicit beauty" and "subjective interest", for I remember not liking the book.

Now I cannot but agree with anyone who judges it to be Stendhal's masterpiece; it has an immediacy of feeling, an obvious sincerity, a remarkable attempt to sweep away accumulated memories and reach the essence. And what lucidity of style! What a mass of reflections, the more precious for being common to all men!

I should like to try and do the same. Indeed it seems obligatory. When one reaches the decline of life it is imperative to try and gather together as many as possible of the sensations which have passed through our particular organism. Few can succeed in thus creating a masterpiece (Rousseau, Stendhal, Proust) but all should find it possible to preserve in some such way things which without this slight effort would be lost for ever. To keep a diary, or write down one's own memories at a certain age, should be a duty "State-imposed"; material thus accumulated would have inestimable value after three or four generations; many of the psychological and historical problems that assail humanity would be resolved. There are no memoirs, even those written by insignificant people, which do not include social and graphic details of first-rate importance.

The extraordinary interest that Defoe's novels aroused is due to the fact that they are near-diaries, brilliant though apocryphal. What, one wonders, would genuine ones have been like? Imagine, say, the diary of a Parisian procuress of the *Régence*, or the memories of Byron's valet during the Venetian period!

I shall try to follow the *Henri Brulard* method as closely as possible, even in describing the "seedlings" of the principal scenes.

But I find I cannot follow Stendhal in "quality" of memory. He interprets his childhood as a time when he was bullied and tyrannised. For me childhood is a lost paradise. Everyone was good to me – I was king of the home – even people later hostile to me were then *"aux petits soins"*.

So the reader (who won't exist) must expect to be led meandering through a lost Earthly Paradise. If it bores him, I don't mind.

II

Casa Lampedusa

First of all, our home. I loved it with utter abandon, and still love it now when for the last twelve years it has been no more than a memory. Until a few months before its destruction I used to sleep in the room where I was born, five yards away from the spot where my mother's bed had stood when she gave me birth. And in that house, in that very room maybe, I was glad to feel a certainty of dying. All my other homes (very few, actually, apart from hotels) have merely been roofs which have served to shelter me from rain and sun, not homes in the traditional and venerable sense of that word. And especially the one I have now, which I don't like at all, which I bought to please my wife and which I'm delighted to have bequeathed to her, because the fact is it's not my house.

So it will be very painful for me to evoke my dead Beloved as she was until 1929 in her integrity and beauty, and as she continued after all to be until 5th April 1943, the day on which bombs brought from beyond the Atlantic searched her out and destroyed her.

The first impression that remains with me is that of her vastness, and this impression owes nothing to the magnifying process which affects all that surrounds one's childhood, but to actual reality. When I saw the area covered by the unsightly ruins I found they were about 1600 square yards in extent. With only ourselves living in one wing, my paternal grandparents in another, my bachelor uncles on the second floor, for twenty years it was all at my disposal, with its three courtyards, four terraces, garden, huge staircases, halls, corridors, stables, little rooms on the *mezzanine* for servants and offices—a real kingdom for a boy alone, a kingdom either empty or sparsely populated by figures unanimously well-disposed.

At no point on earth, I'm sure, has sky ever stretched more violently blue than it did above our enclosed terrace, never has sun thrown gentler rays than those penetrating the half-closed shutters of the "green drawing-room", never have damp-marks on a courtyard's outer walls presented shapes more stimulating to the imagination than those at my home.

I loved everything about it: the irregularity of its walls, the number of its drawing-rooms, the stucco of its ceilings, the nasty smell from my grandparents' kitchen, the scent of violets in my mother's dressing-room, the stuffiness of its stables, the good feel of polished leather in its tack-rooms, the mystery of some unfinished apartments on the top floor, the huge coach-house in which our carriages were kept; a whole world full of sweet mysteries, of surprises ever renewed and ever fresh.

I was its absolute master and would run continually through its vast expanses, climbing the great staircase from the courtyard to the loggia on the roof, from which could be seen the sea and Mount Pellegrino and the whole city as far as Porta Nuova and Monreale. And knowing how by devious routes and turns to avoid inhabited rooms, I would feel alone and dictatorial, followed often only by my friend Tom running excitedly at my heels, with his red tongue dangling from his dear black snout.

The house (and I prefer to call it a house rather than a palace, a word which has been debased in Italy, applied as it is nowadays even to blocks fifteen storeys high), was tucked away in one of the most secluded streets of old Palermo, in Via di Lampedusa, at number 17, the uneven number's evil omen then serving only to add a pleasantly sinister flavour to the joy that it dispensed. (When later the stables were transformed into storerooms we asked for the number to be changed, and it became 23 when the end was near; so number 17 had after all been lucky.)

The street was secluded but not so very narrow, and well paved; nor was it dirty as might be thought, for opposite our entrance and along the whole length of the building extended the old Pietrapersia palace which had no shops or dwellings on the ground floor, its austere, clean front in local white and yellow punctuated by numerous windows protected by enormous grilles, conferring on it the dignified and gloomy air of an old convent or state prison. The bomb explosions later flung many of those heavy grilles into our rooms opposite, with what happy effect on the old stucco work and Murano chandeliers can be imagined.

But if Via di Lampedusa was decent enough, for the whole length of our house at least, the streets into it were not; Via Bara all'Olivella, leading into Piazza Massimo, was crawling with poverty and squalid cellars, and depressing to pass along. It became slightly better when Via Roma was cut through, but there always remained a good stretch of filth and horrors to traverse.

The façade of the house had no particular architectural merit: it was white with wide borders round windows of sulphur yellow, in purest Sicilian style of the seventeenth and eighteenth centuries in fact. It extended along Via di Lampedusa for some seventy yards or so, and had nine big balconies on the front. There were two gateways almost at the corners of the building, of enormous width as they used to be made in olden days to allow carriages to turn in from narrow streets. And in fact there was easy room even for the four-horsed teams which my father drove with mastery to race-meetings at La Favorita.

Just inside the main gate which we always used, the first on the left as one faces the façade, almost at the corner of Via Bara, and separated from the corner of the building by no more than a couple of yards' frontage on to which opened the grilled window of the porter's lodge, one entered a short paved gateway, its two side walls of white stucco supported by a low step. On the left was the porter's nook (which led through to his living quarters), with the fine mahogany door in the middle of which there was a big opaque glass pane with our coat of arms. And immediately after, still on the left preceding the two steps and the entrance to the "grand staircase", with it double-leaved doors also in mahogany and glass (clear this time and devoid of any coat of arms), right in front of the right-hand stairway there was a colonnade of fine grey Billiemi stone that supported the overhanging *tocchetto* or gallery. Beyond this gate in fact lay the main courtyard, cobbled and divided into sections by rows of flagstones. At the far end three great arches, also supported on columns of Billiemi stone, bore a terrace which linked the two wings of the house at that point.

Beneath the first colonnade, to the right of the entrance gates there were several plants, mostly palms, in wooden tubs varnished green, and at the end there was a plaster statue of some Greek god or other, standing. Also at the end, and parallel to the entrance, there was the door to the tack-room.

The main staircase was a very fine one, all in grey Billiemi, with two flights of fifteen steps or so each, set between yellowish walls. Where the second flight began there was a wide oblong landing with two mahogany doors, one facing each flight of stairs; the one giving on to the first flight led to the quarters of the mezzanine devoted to the Administration and called "the Accounts Office", the other to a minute cubby-hole wherein the footmen used to change their livery.

These two doors were decorated with a cornice also in Billiemi of Empire style, and they were surmounted at the height of the first floor each one with bulging little gilt balconies, which both opened on to the little entrance hall to our grandparents' apartments.

I forgot to say that just past the entrance to the stairs, but on the exterior, in the courtyard, hung the red cord of a bell which the porter was supposed to ring in order to warn servants of their mistress's return, or the approach of visitors. The number of rings, which the porters gave with great skill, obtaining, I don't know how, sharp separate strokes without any tiresome tinkling, was rigorously laid down by protocol; four strokes for my grandmother the princess and two for her visitors, three for my mother the duchess and one for her visitors. But misunderstandings would occur, so that when at times my mother, grand-mother and some friend picked up on the way entered in the same carriage a real concert would ring out of four plus three plus two strokes which were never ending. The masters, my grandfather and father, left and returned without any bell ringing for them at all.

The second flight of stairs came out on to the wide luminous *tocchetto*, which was a gallery with the spaces between its columns filled in, for reasons of comfort, by big windows with opaque lozenge-shaped panes. This contained a few sparse pieces of furniture, some big portraits of ancestors, and a large table to the left on which were put letters on arrival (it was then I read a postcard addressed to my uncle Ciccio from Paris, on which some French tart had written: "*Dis à Moffo qu'il est un mufle*"), two pretty chests and a plaster statue of Pandora on the point of opening the fatal box, surrounded by plants. At the end, facing the head of the stairs, there was a door, always closed, which gave directly on to the "green drawing-room" (a door which much later was to become the entrance to our quarters), and to the right of the stairs, the entrance to the "great hall", guarded by an ever-open door, in embroidered red brocade, the upper part displaying our coat of arms and that of the Valdina in colour in the glass.

The "great hall" was immense, flagged in white and grey marble, with three balconies over Via di Lampedusa and one over the Lampedusa courtyard, a dead-end extension of Via Bara. It was divided by an arch which split it in two unequal parts, the first smaller and the second vastly bigger. To my parents' great regret, its decoration was entirely modern, as in 1848 a shell had destroyed the fine painted ceiling and irreparably damaged the wall-frescoes. For a long time, it seems, a fig tree flourished there. The hall was done up when my grandfather married, that is in 1866 or '67, all in white stucco with a wainscot of grey marble. In the centre of the ceiling of each of the two parts a coat of arms was depicted; opposite the entrance there was a big walnut table on which visitors left their hats and capes; then there were a few chests and the odd chair. It was in this great hall that the footmen waited, lounging in their chairs and ready to hurry out into the *tocchetto* at the sound of that bell below.

After coming in by the door in red brocade which I've mentioned, if one turned towards the left-hand wall, one found another door similarly covered but in green, which gave access to our apartment; if one turned left one had to go on through until on the right one reached a little staircase and a door leading to my grandparents' quarters, beginning actually with the "little room" with the two little balconies which overlooked the stairs.

A door with green hangings gave on to the ante-chamber, with six portraits of ancestors hung above its balcony entrance and its two doors, walls of grey silk, and the odd piece of dark furniture. And from there the eye fell on a perspective of drawing-rooms extending one after the other for the length of the façade. Here for me began the magic of light, which in a city with so intense a sun as Palermo is concentrated or variegated according to the weather, even in narrow streets. This light was sometimes diluted by the silk curtains hanging before balconies, or heightened by beating on some gilt frame or yellow damask chair which reflected it back; sometimes, particularly in summer, these rooms were dark, yet through the closed blinds filtered a sense of the luminous power that was outside; or sometimes at certain hours a single ray would penetrate straight and clear as that of Sinai, populated with myriads of dust particles and going to vilify the colours of carpets, uniformly ruby-red throughout all the drawing-rooms: a real sorcery of illumination and colour which entranced my mind for ever. Sometimes I rediscover this luminous quality in some old palace or church, and it would wrench at my heart were I not ready to brush it aside with some "wicked joke".[1]

After the ante-chamber came the *"lambris"* room, so called because its walls were covered half-way up by panelling of inlaid walnut; next the so-called "supper" room, its walls covered with dark flowered orange-coloured silk, part of which still survives as

---

[1] In English in the Italian text. (Trs.)

wall-coverings in my wife's room now. And there was the great
ballroom with its enamelled floor and its ceiling on which
delicious gold and yellow twirls framed mythological scenes
where with rude energy and amid swirling robes crowded all the
deities of Olympus.

After that came my mother's boudoir, very lovely, its ceiling
scattered with flowers and branches of old coloured stucco, in a
design gentle and corporeal as a piece of music by Mozart.

And after that one entered my mother's bedroom, which was
very big; the principal wall where[1] there was the room at the
corner of the house with a balcony (the last one) on Via
Lampedusa, and one on the garden of the oratory of Santa Zita.
The decorations in wood, stucco and paint in this room were
among the finest in the house.

From the drawing-room known as the "*lambris*" room, going
left one entered the "green drawing-room", which led into the
"yellow drawing-room", and hence into a room which started
out as my day-nursery, later to be turned into a little red drawing-
room, the room which we most frequented, and which later
became a library. This place had on the left (entering from the
yellow drawing-room) a window on to the great courtyard and
in the same wall a glass-panelled door giving on to the terrace. At
right angles with these openings there was first a door (later
bricked up) which led into a little room which used to be my
grandfather's bathroom (it even had a marble bathtub) and which
served as repository for my toys, and another glass-panelled door
giving on to the small terrace.

[1] The Italian text here appears to be corrupted. (Trs.)

III

The Journey

But the house in Palermo had dependencies in the country which multiplied its charms. These were four; Santa Margherita Belice, a villa at Bagherìa, a palace at Torretta and a country house at Raitano. Then there was also the old home of the family at Palma and the castle of Montechiaro, but to those we never went.

The favourite was Santa Margherita, in which we would spend long months even of winter. It was one of the loveliest country houses I have ever seen. Built in 1680, it had been completely restored about 1810 by Prince Cutò on the occasion of a long sojourn there made by Ferdinand IV and Maria Carolina, forced to reside in Sicily during the years Murat was reigning in Naples. Afterwards, though, it had not been abandoned as were all other houses in Sicily, but constantly looked after, restored and enriched until the days of my grandmother Cutò, who, having lived in France until the age of twenty, had not inherited the Sicilian aversion for country life; she was in residence there almost continuously and brought it "up-to-date" (for the Second Empire, of course, which was not very different from the general standard of comfort throughout Europe until 1914).

The charm of adventure, of the not wholly comprehensible, which is so much part of my memories of Santa Margherita, began with the journey there. This was an enterprise full of discomforts and delights. At that time there were no automobiles; around 1905 the only one that circulated around Palermo was old Signora Giovanna Florio's "*électrique*". A train left the Lolli railway station at ten past five in the morning. So we had to get up at half past three. Awakening at that hour was always nasty and made all the more miserable for me by the fact that it was the time at which I was given castor oil when I had stomach-ache. Servants and cooks had already left the day before. We were bundled into two closed landaus: in the first my father and mother, the governess Anna I, let's say, and myself; in the second Teresa, or Concettina maybe, my mother's maid, Ferrara, our accountant, a native of Santa Margherita and coming to spend the holidays with his family, and Paolo, my father's valet. Another vehicle followed I think, with luggage and hampers for luncheon.

It was usually about the end of June and dawn would be just spreading over the deserted streets. Across Piazza Politeama and Via Dante (then called Via Esposizione) we reached the Lolli railway station, where we packed into the train for Trapani. Trains then had no corridors, and so no lavatories; and when I was very small there was brought along for my use a chamber-pot in ghastly brown china bought on purpose and flung out of the window before reaching our destination. The ticket-collector would do his rounds by grappling along the exterior of the carriages, and all at once we would see his braided cap and black-gloved hand rising outside.

For hours then we crossed the lovely, desperately sad landscape of western Sicily; it must have been I think just exactly the same as Garibaldi's Thousand had found it on landing – Carini, Cinisi, Zucco, Partinico; then the line went along the sea, the rails seeming laid on the sand itself; the sun, already hot, was broiling us in our iron box. Thermos flasks did not exist, and there were no refreshments to be expected at any station. The train next cut inland, among stony hills and fields of mown corn, yellow as the manes of lions. Eventually at eleven we reached Castelvetrano, then far from being the spry, thrusting little town it is now; it was a dreary place, with open drains and pigs walking in the main street; and flies by the billion. At the station, which had already been roasting under the sun for six hours, were waiting our carriages, two landaus fitted with yellow curtains.

At half past eleven we set off again; for an hour as far as Partanna the road was level and easy, across fine, cultivated country; we began to recognise places we knew, a pair of majolica negroes' heads on the entrance pillars of a villa, an iron cross commemorating a murder; as we drew closer beneath Partanna, however, the scene changed: three Carabinieri appeared, a sergeant and two troopers on horseback, the napes of their necks protected by patches of white stuff like horsemen in Fattori's pictures, who were to accompany us all the way to Santa Margherita. The road became mountainous: around us unrolled the immeasurable scenery of feudal Sicily, desolate, breathless, oppressed by a leaden sun. We looked about for a tree under whose shade to lunch; but there were only scraggy olives which gave no shelter from the sun. Eventually an abandoned peasant's hut was found, half in ruins, but its windows carefully closed. In its shade we alighted and ate; succulent things mostly. Slightly apart, the Carabinieri, who had bread, meat, cakes and bottles sent over to them, made a gay luncheon of their own, untroubled by the burning sun. At the end of the meal the sergeant would come up holding a brimming glass: "I thank Your Excellencies on behalf of myself and my men!" And he took a gulp of wine which must have had a temperature of 104 degrees.

But one of the soldiers had remained on foot watchfully prowling round the hut.

Back we got into the carriages. It was now two o'clock – the truly ghastly hour of the Sicilian countryside in summer. We were moving at walking pace, for the slope down towards the Belice river was now starting. All were silent, and the only sound to be heard through the stamp of hooves was the voice of a Carabiniere humming "*La Spagnola sa amar cosi*".[1] Dust rose. Then we were across the Belice, a real and proper river for Sicily – it even had water in its bed – and began the interminable ascent at walking pace; bend succeeded bend eternally in the chalky landscape.

It seemed never-ending, and yet it did end. At the top of the slope the horses stopped, steaming with sweat; the Carabinieri

---

[1] "That's how a Spanish woman loves." (Trs.)

dismounted, we too alighted to stretch our legs. Then we set off again at a trot.

My mother was now beginning to warn me.

"Watch out now, soon on the left we'll see La Venaría."

In fact we were now passing over a bridge, and there on the left at last glimpsed a little verdure, some bamboo, even a patch or so of orange-grove. This was Le Dàgali, the first Cutò property on our road. And behind Le Dàgali was a steep hill, traversed to the top by a wide alley of cypresses leading to La Venaría, a hunting lodge of ours.

We were not far off now. My mother, on tenterhooks because of her love for Santa Margherita, could no longer sit still and kept on craning out of one window or another. "We're nearly at Montevago." "We're home!" Across Montevago we drove, first nucleus of life seen after four hours on the road. What a nucleus though! Wide deserted streets, houses weighed down equally by poverty and by implacable sun, not a living soul, only a few pigs and some cats' carcasses.

But once past Montevago everything improved. The road was straight and level, the countryside smiling. "There's the Giambalvo villa! There's the Madonna of Graces and its cypresses!" and she even hailed the cemetery with delight. Then the Madonna of Trapani. "We've arrived – there's the bridge!"

It was five in the afternoon. We had been travelling for twelve hours. On the bridge were lined up the municipal band, which broke into a lively polka. Exhausted as we were, with eyebrows white from dust and throats parched, we forced ourselves to smile and thank. A short drive through the streets and we came out into the piazza, saw the graceful lines of our home, and entered its gateway; first courtyard, passageway, second courtyard. We had arrived. At the bottom of the external staircase stood a little group of retainers, headed by our excellent agent Don Nofrio, tiny beneath his white beard and flanked by his powerful wife. "Welcome!" "We're so pleased to have arrived!"

Up in one of the drawing-rooms Don Nofrio had prepared crushed ice and lemon drinks, badly made but a blessing all the same. I was dragged off by Anna to my room and plunged, reluctant, into a tepid bath which the agent, peerless man, had thought of having ready, while my wretched parents faced the hordes of acquaintances already beginning to arrive.

IV

The House

Set in the middle of the town, right on the leafy square, it spread over a vast expanse and contained about a hundred rooms, large and small. It gave the impression of an enclosed and self-sufficient entity, of a kind of Vatican as it were, that included state-rooms, living-rooms, quarters for thirty guests, servants' rooms, three great courtyards, stables and coach-houses, a private theatre and church, a large and very lovely garden, and a big orchard.

And what rooms they were! Prince Niccolò had had the good taste, almost unique for his time, not to ruin the eighteenth-century salons. In the state apartments every door was framed on both sides by fantastic friezes in grey, black or red marble, whose harmonious asymmetry sounded a gay fanfare at everyone passing from one room to another. From the second courtyard a wide balustraded staircase of green marble, in a single flight, led up to a terrace on which opened the great entrance doors, surmounted by the belled cross of the Cutò arms.

These led into a broad entrance hall, its walls entirely covered with two ranks, one above the other, of pictures representing the Filangeri family from 1080 until my grandmother's father; all lifesize standing figures in a great variety of costume, from a Crusader's to a Gentleman's-in-Waiting to Ferdinand II, pictures which in spite of their mediocre workmanship filled the big room with lively familiar presences. Beneath each, in white letters on a black background, were written their names and titles, and the chief events of their lives. "Riccardo, defended Antioch against the Infidels." "Raimondo, wounded in the defence of Acre"; another Riccardo, "chief instigator of the Sicilian Revolt" (that is, of the Sicilian Vespers), Niccolò I "led two Hussar regiments against the Gallic hordes in 1796".

Above each door or window, however, there were the panoramic maps of the "fiefs", then still almost all present and correct. In all four corners were bronze statues of warriors in armour, a concession to the taste of the period, each holding on high a simple oil lamp. On the ceiling Jupiter, wrapped in a lilac cloud, blessed the embarkation of Roger as he prepared to sail from his native Normandy for Sicily; and tritons and water-nymphs frolicked around galleys ready to set forth on mother-of-pearl seas.

Once this proud overture was passed though, the house was all grace and charm, or rather gentleness veiled its pride as courtesy does that of an aristocrat. There was a library, its books shut inside cupboards of that decorative eighteenth-century Sicilian style called "Monastic", not unlike the more florid Venetian, but cruder and less sweetened. There was nearly every work of the Enlightenment in tawny leather and gilt binding: *L'Encyclopédie*, Fontenelle, Helvétius, Voltaire in Kehl's great edition. (If Maria Carolina read that, what must she have thought?), then *Victoires et Conquêtes*, a collection of Napoleonic bulletins and campaign reports which were my delight in the long silence-filled summer afternoons as I read them sprawled on one of those over-large "poufs" which occupied the centre of the ballroom. An odd library, in fact, if one considers that it had been formed by a man as reactionary as that Prince Niccolò. Also to be found there were bound collections of the satirical journals of the Risorgimento, *Il Fischietto* and *Lo Spirito Folletto*, some exquisite editions of Don Quixote, of La Fontaine, that rare history of Napoleon with Norvins' charming illustrations (a book I still have); and among moderns the complete works, or almost, of Zola, whose yellow covers showed up glaringly on that mellow background, and a few other lesser novels; but there was also *I Malavoglia*, with an autographed dedication.

*   *   *

I do not know whether I have managed so far to convey the idea that I was a boy who loved solitude, who liked the company of things more than of people. This being the case it will easily be understood how ideal for me was life at Santa Margherita. I would wander through the vast ornate house (twelve people in three hundred rooms) as in an enchanted wood. A wood with no hidden dragons, full of happy marvels, even in the jesting names of the rooms: the "aviary" room, its walls covered in rough crinkled white silk, on which amid infinite festoons of flowering branches glittered tiny multi-coloured birds painted in by hand; the "*ouistiti*" room where on similar tropical trees swung sly and hairy monkeys; "the rooms of Ferdinando" which evoked at first in me the idea of a fair smiling uncle of mine, but which had actually kept this name because they had been the private apartments of the cruel and jocular *Re Nasone*, as was also shown by the huge Empire "*lit-bateau*", whose mattress was covered in a kind of morocco leather casing, apparently used on royal beds instead of an under blanket; green morocco leather, closely stamped with the triple gilt lilies of Bourbon, and looking like an enormous book. The walls were covered in silk of paler green, with vertical stripes, one shiny and one mat with tiny lines, just like the one in the green drawing-room of our house in Palermo. Then in the "tapestry hall', the only one with some sinister association later, hung eight big tapestries on subjects taken from *Gerusalemme Liberata*. In one of these, representing an equestrian joust between Tancredi and Argante, one of the two horses had a strangely human look which I was to link in my mind later with Poe's *House of the Metzengersteins*. This particular tapestry, actually, is still in my possession.

The evenings, oddly enough, we always spent in the ballroom, an apartment in the centre of the first floor with eight balconies looking out over the piazza and four over the first courtyard. It was reminiscent of the ballroom of our house in Palermo; here, too, gold was the dominating note of the room. The walls, on the other hand, were pale green, almost entirely covered with hand-embroidered flowers and golden leaves, and the bases of pillars and the shutters vast as front doors were covered completely in dull gold-leaf with decorations in brighter gold. And when on winter evenings (we actually spent two winters at Santa Margherita, which my mother was loth to leave) we sat in front of the central fireplace, by the glow of a few petrol lamps whose light picked out capriciously a few flowers on the walls and flames in the shutters, we seemed to be enclosed in some magician's cave. I can definitely place the date of one of these evenings because I remember that newspapers were brought in announcing the fall of Port Arthur.

These evenings were not always restricted to the family alone; in fact they seldom were. My mother wanted to keep up her parents' tradition of being on cordial terms with the local notables, and many of these would dine with us in turn, while twice a week everyone met to play *scopone* in the ballroom. My mother had known them since childhood and liked them all; to me they seemed what perhaps they were not, good people without exception. Among them there was a native of Palermo forced by his wretched financial condition to emigrate to Santa Margherita, where he had a tiny house and an even tinier patch of ground; he was a practised shot, had been a close friend of my grandfather's, and enjoyed particularly favourable treatment; I think he used to lunch with us every day and was the only one to call my mother *"tu"*, which she returned with a respectful *"lei"*. He was a straight-backed, wiry old man, with blue eyes and long white sprouting moustaches, distinguished and even elegant in his well-cut if threadbare clothes. I suspect now that he may have been a bastard of the Cutò family, some uncle of my mother's in fact. He would play the piano and tell wonderful tales of shooting out in the wilds and woods with my grandfather, of the prodigious acumen of his gun-dogs (Diana and Furetta) and of alarming but ever innocuous encounters with the brigand bands of Leone and Capraro. Then there was Nenè Giaccone, a big local landowner, with his flamboyant little goatee and insatiable vivacity; he was highly esteemed in the town as a great *viveur*

because he spent two months of every year in Palermo at the
Hotel Milano, on Via Emerico Amari, opposite the side façade of
the Politeama – this was considered fast.

There was the Cavaliere Mario Rossi, a little man with a small
black beard; he was an old post-office clerk who talked of nothing
but Frascati ("You must realise, duchess, that Frascati is almost
Rome") where his duties had taken him for a few months. There
was Ciccio Neve, with his big rubicund face and mutton-chop
whiskers à la Franz-Josef, who lived with a mad sister (when one
knows a Sicilian village well one discovers innumerable lunatics);
there was Catania the schoolmaster, bearded like Moses; and
another landowner, Montalbano, the typical rustic lordling,
obtuse and gross, the father, I believe, of the present Communist
member of Parliament; Giorgio di Giuseppe, the intellectual of
the company, from beneath whose windows passers-by at night
heard him playing Chopin's nocturnes on the piano; Giambalvo,
hugely fat and full of fun; Doctor Monteleone with a little black
beard, who had studied in Paris and often spoke of the Rue
Monge where he had had the oddest adventures; Don Colicchio
Terrasa, very old and almost wholly peasant, with his son Totò, a
great trencherman; and many others who were seen more rarely.

It will be noticed these were one and all men. Wives, daughters,
sisters stayed at home, both because women in the country (in
1905–14) did not pay social calls, and also because their husbands,
fathers and brothers did not consider them presentable. My
mother and father would go and visit them once a season, and
with Mario Rossi, whose wife was a Bilella and famous for her
gastronomic arts, they would even take luncheon now and again;
sometimes after a complex system of signals and warnings, she
would send over by a small boy, who came galloping across the
piazza under the broiling sun, an immense tureen full of macaroni
done with barley in the Sicilian mode with chopped meat, egg-
plant and basil, which was, I remember, truly a dish fit for rustic
and primitive gods. The boy had precise orders to set this on the
dining table when we were already sitting down and, before
leaving, he would say: "'*A signura raccumanna: 'u cascavaddu*"

("The signora recommends: cacciocavallo cheese"); an injunction perhaps sage but never obeyed.

The one exception to this absence of women was Margherita, the daughter of Nenè Giaccone the *viveur*; a pretty girl with auburn hair like her father, she had been educated at the Sacred Heart and was to be seen every now and then.

In contrast to the cordial relations with the townsfolk, those with the authorities were strained; the Mayor, Don Pietro Giaccone, was not on the visiting list, and neither was the parish priest, for all that the Cutò family had the benefice in their gift. The Mayor's absence is explained by the continuous feuding with the Town Hall over "civic customs". The Mayor was also a ladies' man and for a while he kept a trollop who passed herself off for a Spaniard, Pepita; he had unearthed her in a café-concert at Agrigento (!) and she drove about the streets of the town in a trap drawn by a grey pony. One day, as my father was standing outside the front entrance, he saw the couple passing in their elegant equipage; and with the unerring eye he had for these things he noticed that the wheel-hub had come away from its mounting and the wheel was on the point of falling off; so although he was not acquainted with the Mayor and their relations were strained, he ran after the trap shouting: "Cavaliere look out, your right wheel's coming off."

The Mayor stopped, saluted with his whip and said: "Thank you. I'll see to it." And he resumed his way without dismounting. Another twenty yards and the wheel did indeed go off after its own purposes, and the Mayor was rudely thrown to the ground together with Pepita in her pink chiffon dress. They were but slightly hurt. The following day four partridges arrived and a visiting card: "Cav. Pietro Giaccone, Mayor of Santa Margherita Belice, to thank for the good but unheeded advice." But this symptom of a thaw had no sequel.

V

The Garden

In the Santa Margherita house, the last and biggest of the three courtyards was the "courtyard of the palms"; it was planted all over with the tallest of palm trees which in that season were laden with clusters of unfertilised dates. Entering it from the passage leading from the second courtyard, one had on one's right the long and low line of the building that housed the stables with, beyond it, the riding-school. In the centre of the courtyard, to the left of the stables and riding-school, stood two high pillars in porous yellow stone, adorned with masks and scrolls, which opened on to flights of steps leading down into the garden. They were short flights (a dozen or so steps in all) but in that space the baroque architect had found ways of expressing a freakish and whimsical turn of mind, alternating high and low steps, subjecting the flights to the most unexpected distortions, creating superfluous little landings with niches and benches so as to produce in this small space a variety of possible joinings and separations, of brusque rejections and affectionate reconciliations, which imparted to the staircase the atmosphere of a lovers' tiff.

The garden, like so many others in Sicily, was designed on a level lower than the house, I think so that advantage could be taken of a spring welling up there. It was very large and, when seen from a window of the house, perfectly regular in its complicated system of alleys and paths. It was all planted out with ilex and araucaria, the alleys bordered with myrtle hedges; and in the furnace of summer, when the jet of the spring dwindled, it was a paradise of parched scents of origanum and calamint, as are

33

so many gardens in Sicily that seem made to delight the nose rather than the eyes.

The long alleys surrounding it on all four sides were the only straight ones in the whole garden, for in the rest the designer (who must surely have been the whimsical architect of the stairs) had multiplied twists, turns, mazes and corridors, contributing to give it that tone of graceful mystery which enveloped the whole house. All these cross-alleys, however, came out eventually on to a big central clearing, the one where the spring had been found; this, now enclosed in an ornate prison, lightened with its spurts a great fountain in the centre of which, on an islet of artificial ruins, a dishevelled and ungirt goddess of Abundance poured torrents of water into a deep basin forever crossed by friendly ripples. It was bounded by a balustrade, surmounted here and there by tritons and nereids sculptured in the act of diving with movements that were disordered in each individual statue but fused into a scenic whole. All round the fountain were stone benches, darkened by centuries-old moss, protected from sun and wind by a tangle of foliage.

But for a child the garden was brim full of surprises. In a corner was a big conservatory filled with cacti and rare shrubs, the kingdom of Nino, head gardener and my great friend, he, too, redhaired like so many at Santa Margherita, perhaps owing to the Norman Filangeri. There was a bamboo thicket, growing thick and sturdy around a secondary fountain, in the shade of which was an open space for games, with a swing from which long before my time Pietro Scalea, later Minister of War, fell and broke his arm. In one of the side alleys, embedded in the wall, was a big cage destined at one time for monkeys, in which my cousin Clementina Trigona and I shut ourselves one day, a Sunday morning when the garden was open to the townsfolk who stopped in mute amazement to gaze, uncertainly, at these dressed-up simians. There was a "dolls' house", built for the diversion of my mother and her four sisters, made of red brick, with window frames in *pietra serena*; now, with its roof and floors fallen in, it was the only disconsolate corner of the big garden, the remainder of which Nino kept in admirable order with every tree well pruned, every alley yellow-pebbled, every bush clipped.

Every two weeks or so a cart came up from the nearby Belice with a big barrel full of eels, which were unloaded into the secondary fountain (the one of the bamboos), that served as a fishpond, when the cook sent for them to be scooped out with little nets according to the needs of the kitchen.

Everywhere at corners of alleys rose figures of obscure gods, usually noseless; and as in every self-respecting Eden there was a serpent hidden in the shadows, in the shape of some castor-oil shrubs (lovely in other ways with their oblong green leaves bordered in red) which one day gave me a nasty surprise when, crushing the berries of a fine vermilion bunch, I recognised upon the air the smell of the oil that, at that happy age, was the only real shadow on my life. My beloved Tom was following me, and I held out my besmirched hand for him to sniff; I still can see the kindly and reproachful way in which he puckered half of his black lip, as well brought-up dogs do when they want to show their disgust without giving offence to their masters.

A garden, I have said, full of surprises. But the whole of Santa Margherita was that, full of cheerful little traps. One would open a door on a passage and glimpse a perspective of rooms dim in the shade of half-pulled shutters, their walls covered with French prints representing Bonaparte's campaigns in Italy; at the top of the stairs leading to the second floor was a door that was almost invisible, so narrow was it and flush with the wall, and behind this was a big room crammed with old pictures hung right up to the very top of the walls, as in prints of the Paris *Salon* in the eighteenth century. One of the ancestral portraits in the first room was hinged, and behind lay my grandfather's gun-rooms, for he was a great shot.

The trophies shut in glass cabinets were local only: crimson-footed partridges, disconsolate-looking woodcock, coots from the Belice; but a big bench with scales, little measures for preparing cartridges, glass-fronted cupboards full of multi-

coloured cartridge-cases, coloured prints showing more dangerous adventures (I can still see a bearded explorer in white fleeing
screaming before the charge of a greenish rhinoceros), all these
were enchantments to an adolescent. On the walls also hung
prints and photographs of gun-dogs, pointers and setters,
showing the calm of all canine faces. The guns were ranged in big
racks, ticketed with numbers corresponding to a register in which
were recorded the shots fired from each. It was from one of these
guns, I think a lady's, with two richly damascened barrels, that I
fired, in the garden, the first and last shots of my sporting career;
one of the bearded keepers forced me to shoot at some innocent
redbreasts; two fell, unfortunately, with blood on their tepid grey
plumage; and as they were still quivering the keeper wrung their
necks with his fingers.

In spite of my readings of "*Victoires et Conquêtes*", and "*L'épée
de l'intrépide général comte Delort rougie du sang des ennemis de
l'Empire*" this scene horrified me: apparently I only like blood
when metamorphosed into printer's ink. I went straight to my
father, to whose orders this slaughter of the Innocents was due,
and said that never again would I fire on any creature.

Ten years later I was to kill a Bosnian with a pistol and who
knows how many other Christians by shellfire. But this never
made on me a tenth of the impression left by those two wretched
robins.

There was also the "carriage-room", a great, dark chamber, in
which stood two enormous eighteenth-century *carrosses*, one
gala, all gilt and glass, with doors on whose panels, against a
yellow background, were painted pastoral scenes in "*vernis
Martin*"; its seats, for at least six persons, were of faded taffeta; the
other, a travelling carriage, was olive-green with gilt edgings and
coats-of-arms on the door panels, and was upholstered in green
Morocco leather. Beneath the seats there were lined cupboards
intended, I think, for provisions on a journey, but now containing
only a solitary silver dish.

Then there was the "children's kitchen" with a miniature range
and a set of copper cooking implements to scale, which my

grandmother had installed in a vain attempt to inveigle her daughters into learning to cook.

And then there was the church and the theatre, with the fairy-tale passages by which they were reached, but of those I will speak later.

Amid all these splendours I slept in a completely bare room overlooking the garden, called the "pink room" because of the colour of its varnished plaster; on one side was a dressing-room with a strange oval brass bath raised on four high wooden legs. I remember the baths which I was made to take in water that had starch dissolved in it or bran in a little bag from which when wet came a scented, milky drip; *bains de son*, bran baths, traces of which can be found in memoirs of the Second Empire, a habit which had evidently been handed on to my mother by my grandmother.

In a room nearby, identical to mine, but blue, slept a succession of governesses, Anna I and Anna II, who were German, and Mademoiselle, who was French. At my bedhead hung a kind of Louis Seize showcase in white wood, enclosing three ivory statuettes of the Holy Family on a crimson background. This case has been miraculously salvaged and now hangs at the bedhead of the room in which I sleep at my cousin Piccolo's villa at Capo d'Orlando. In that villa, too, I retrieve not only the "Holy Family" of my infancy, but a trace, faint certainly but unmistakable, of my childhood; and so I love going there.

VI

The Church and the Theatre

There was also the church, which was then the cathedral of Santa Margherita. From the carriage-room one turned left and, up a few steps, reached a wide passage ending in a kind of school-room with benches, blackboards, and relief maps, where my mother and aunts had done their lessons as children.

It was at Santa Margherita, at the not-so-tender age of eight, that I was taught to read. To begin with, others read aloud to me; on alternate days, that is Tuesdays, Thursdays and Saturdays, "Sacred History" and a kind of potted version of the Bible and the Gospels; and on Mondays, Wednesdays and Fridays, classical mythology. So I acquired a "solid" knowledge of both these disciplines; I am still capable of saying how many, and who, were the brothers of Joseph and of finding my way among the complicated family squabbles of the Atrides. Before I learnt to read for myself my grandmother was forced by her own goodness to read aloud for an hour from *The Queen of the Caribbean* by Salgari; and I can still see her trying hard not to fall asleep as she read out about the prowess of the Black Pirate and the swashbuckling of Carmaux.

Eventually it was decided that this religious, classic, and adventuresome culture, vicariously imparted, could not last much longer, and that I was to be handed over to Donna Carmela, an elementary schoolmistress at Santa Margherita. Nowadays elementary schoolmistresses are smart lively young ladies, who chatter about Pestalozzi's and James's pedagogic studies and want to be called "*Professoressa*". In 1905, in Sicily, an elementary schoolmistress was an old woman more than half-peasant, with her spectacled head wrapped up in a black shawl; but actually this one was a most expert teacher, and within two months I knew how to read and write and had lost my doubts about double consonants and accented syllables. For whole weeks, in the "blue room" separated from my pink room only by the passage, I had to carry out articulated dictations – ar-ti-cu-la-ted dic-ta-tions – and repeat dozens of times, "di, do, da, fo, fa, fu, *qui* and *qua* don't take an accent." Blessed labours! Thanks to them it will never be my lot, as it has been the lot of a distinguished senator, to be surprised at the frequency with which newspapers and handbills incur the error of slipping an extra b into "Republic".

When I had learnt to write Italian my mother taught me to write French; I already spoke it and had often been to Paris and in France, but it was now that I learnt to read French. I can still see my mother sitting with me at a desk, writing slowly and very clearly *le chien, le chat, le cheval* in the columns of an exercise book with a shiny blue cover, and teaching me that what the French pronounce as "ch" the Italians pronounce as "sh", "like 'scirocco and Sciacca'", she would say. From then on, until my school-days, I spent all my afternoons in my grandparents' apartments at Via di Lampedusa, reading behind a screen. At five o'clock my grandfather would call me into his study to give me my afternoon refreshment – a hunk of hard bread and a large glass of cold water. This has remained my favourite drink ever since.

Before reaching the school-room there were two doors on the left which led to three guest-rooms; these were most favoured because they gave on to the terrace on which the entrance stairway abutted. On the right of the carriage-room, between two white console tables, was a big yellow door. From this one entered a small oblong room, its chairs and various tables loaded with images of Saints; I can still see a big china dish in the middle of which lay the head of St John the Baptist, life-size, with blood coagulated in the bottom. From this room one entered a gallery at the level of a high first storey, looking straight on to the High

Altar, which was surrounded by a superb railing of flowery gilt. In this gallery were prie-dieux, chairs, and innumerable rosaries, and from it every Sunday at eleven we attended High Mass, sung without excessive fervour. The church itself was a fine spacious one, I remember, in Empire style, with large, ugly frescoes in white stucco work on the ceiling, as in the Olivella church in Palermo which it resembled, albeit on a smaller scale.

From this same carriage-room which, I now remember, was a kind of revolving stage for the least frequented part of the house, one penetrated to the right into a series of passages, cubby-holes and staircases that gave one a sense of having no outlet, like certain dreams – and eventually reached the corridor of the theatre. This was a real and proper theatre, with two tiers each of twelve boxes, as well as a main box and, of course, the stalls. The auditorium, capable of holding at least three hundred people, was all white and gold, with its seats and the walls of boxes lined in very light blue velvet. The style was Louis Seize, restrained and elegant. In the centre was the equivalent of the royal box, that is, our box, surmounted by an enormous shield of gilt wood, containing the belled cross set on a double-headed eagle's breast. And the drop-curtain, rather later in date, represented the defence of Antioch by Riccardo Filangeri (a defence which, according to Grousset, was far less heroic than the painter gave one to believe).

The auditorium was lit by gilt petrol lamps set on brackets projecting under the first tier of boxes.

The best of it was that this theatre (which of course also had a public entrance from the piazza) was often used.

Every now and again a company of actors would arrive; these were strolling players who, generally in summer, moved on carts from one village to the other, staying two or three days in each to give performances. In Santa Margherita where there was a proper theatre they stayed longer, two or three weeks.

At ten in the morning the leading actor would call in frock-coat and top hat to ask for permission to perform in the theatre; he would be received by my father or, in his absence, by my mother, who of course gave permission, refused any rent (or rather made a contract for a token rental of fifty *centesimi* for the two weeks), and also paid a subscription for our own box. After which the leading actor left, to return half-an-hour later and request a loan of furniture. These companies travelled, in fact, with a few bits of painted scenery but no stage furniture, which would have been too costly and inconvenient to carry about. The furniture was granted, and in the evening we would recognise our armchairs, tables and wardrobes on the stage (they were not our best, I'm sorry to say). They were handed back punctually at the moment of departure, sometimes so garishly revarnished that we had to ask other companies to desist from this well-intentioned practice. Once, if I remember right, the leading lady also called on us, a fat good-natured Ferrarese of about thirty who was to play *La Dame aux Camélias* for the closing night. Finding her own wardrobe unsuitable for the solemnity of the occasion she came to ask my mother for an evening dress: and so the Lady of the Camellias appeared in a very low-cut robe of Nile green covered in silver spangles.

These companies wandering round country villages have now vanished, which is a pity. The scenery was primitive, the acting obviously bad; but they played with gusto and fire and their "presence" was certainly more life-like than are the pallid shades of fifth-rate films now shown in the same villages.

Every night there was a play, and the repertoire was most extensive; the whole of nineteenth-century drama passed on that stage; Scribe, Rovetta, Sardou, Giacometti and Torelli. Once there was even a *Hamlet*, the first time in fact that I ever heard it. And the audience, partly of peasants, were attentive and warm in their applause. At Santa Margherita, at least, these companies did good business, with theatre and furniture free and their draught-horses put up and foddered in our stables.

I used to attend every night, except on one night of the season called "black night", when some French *pochade*, reputed indecent, was shown. Next day our local friends came to report on this libertine performance, and were usually very disappointed as they had expected something much more salacious.

I enjoyed it all enormously, and so did my parents. The better companies at the end of their season were offered a kind of rustic garden party with a simple but abundant buffet out in the garden, which cheered up the stomachs, often empty I fear, of those excellent strolling players.

But already in the last year in which I spent a long period at Santa Margherita, 1921, companies of actors no longer came, and instead flickering films were shown. The war had killed off, among others, these poor and picturesque wandering companies which had their own artistic merits and were, I have an idea, the training school of many a great Italian actor and actress of the nineteenth century, Duse among others.

VII

Excursions

Of all the walks around Santa Margherita, that towards
Montevago was our most frequent, for it ran level, was the right
length (about two miles each way), and had a definite if not
attractive goal; Montevago itself.

Then there was a walk in the opposite direction, on the main
road towards Misilbesi; one passed under a huge umbrella pine
and then over the Dragonara bridge, surrounded unexpectedly
by thick, wild verdure which reminded me of scenes from
Ariosto as I imagined them at that period from Doré's illustrations. The landscape around Misilbesi had a ruffianly air about
it suggestive of violence and hardship of a sort I imagined was
no longer to be found in Sicily; a few years ago I noticed a by-
road near Santa Ninfa (called Rampinzeri) in which I recognised
the same ruffianly yet amiable aspect I associated with Misilbesi.
On reaching Misilbesi, a sunbaked cross-roads marked by an old
house with three dusty and deserted tracks that seemed to be
leading to Hades rather than to Sciacca or Sambuca, we generally
returned by carriage as our usual four miles were by then greatly
exceeded.

The carriage had followed us at walking pace, stopping every
now and again so as not to overtake us and then rejoining us
unhurriedly; phases of silence and of disappearance alternating
according to the turns of the road, before we were caught up with
a clatter.

In autumn our walks had as goal the vineyard of Toto Ferrara,
where we would sit on stones and eat the sweetest mottled grapes
(vine grapes, for in 1905 table grapes were scarcely ever cultivated

The little shrine at the other side of the open space in the gardens was a target for anti-clerical manifestos by Santa Margherita's law students, there on vacation. Often could be seen written up in pencil strophes from Carducci's "Hymn to Satan": "*Salute, o Satana, o ribellione, o forza vindice della ragione.*"[1] And when my mother (who knew the "Hymn to Satan" by heart and whose lack of admiration for it was due to aesthetic reasons alone) next morning sent Nino our gardener to put a coat of whitewash over the modestly sacrilegious verses, others appeared two days later: "*Ti scomunico, o prete, vate di lutti e d'ire*"[2] and other volleys which the good Giosuè[3] thought it his duty to discharge against citizen Mastai.[4]

On the slope below the kiosk could be gathered capers, which I did regularly at the risk of breaking my neck; and around there also, it seems, were to be found those Spanish flies whose pulverised heads make such a potent aphrodisiac. I was sure at the time that these flies were there; but whom I heard this from, or when or how, remains a mystery. Never in my life, at any rate, have I set eyes on Spanish flies, dead or alive, whole or in powder.

Such were our daily, not very exacting, walks. Then there were longer, more complicated ones, our excursions.

The chief excursion of all was that to La Venaría, a hunting lodge on a spur just before Montevago. This was an excursion always made with local guests twice or so in a season, and was never without an element of comedy. A decision would be reached: "Next Sunday, lunch at Venaría". And in the morning off we would set at ten o'clock, ladies in carriages, men on donkeys. Although all or almost all the men owned horses or at least mules, the use of donkeys was traditional; the only rebel was my father, who got round the difficulty by declaring himself to be the one person capable of driving, on those roads, the dog-cart

---

[1] "Greetings, oh Satan, oh rebellion, oh avenging force of reason."
[2] "I excommunicate you, oh priest, prophet mourning and wrath."
[3] Carducci.
[4] Pope Pius IX.

conveying the ladies and bearing also in the dog-cages secreted under the box, bottles and cakes for the guests' luncheon.

Amid laughter and jest the company would take the road to Montevago. In the middle of the dusty group was the dog-cart in which my mother, with Anna or whichever Mademoiselle was with us, Margherita Giaccone and some other lady, tried to shelter from the dust with grey veils of almost Moslem thickness; around would prance the donkeys (or rather "'*i scecche*", for in Sicilian donkeys are almost always feminine, like ships in English) their ears flapping. There were real falls, genuine donkeys' mutinies, and pretended falls due to love of the picturesque. We crossed Montevago, arousing vocal protests from every dog in the place, reached the Dàgari bridge, dropped down into the adjacent depression and began climbing.

The avenue was really grandiose; about three hundred yards long, it went straight up towards the top of the hill, bordered on each side by a double row of cypresses; not adolescent cypresses like those of San Guido, but great trees[1] almost a hundred years old, whose thick branches spread their austere scent in every season. The rows of trees were interrupted every now and again by sets of benches, and once by a fountain with a great mask emitting water at intervals. Under the odorous shade we climbed towards La Venaría, bathed in full sunshine high above.

It was a hunting lodge built at the end of the eighteenth century, considered "tiny", though actually it must have had at least twenty rooms. Built on top of the hill, on the opposite side to the one by which we approached, it looked sheer across the valley, the same valley to be seen from the public gardens, which from higher up seemed vast and even desolate.

Cooks had left that morning at seven and had already prepared everything; when a boy look-out announced the group's approach they thrust into the ovens their famous *timbales* of macaroni *alla Talleyrand*, (the only macaroni which keeps for a period), so that when we arrived we had scarcely time to wash our

---

[1] Now felled by later owners.

hands before going straight out on to the terrace, where two tables had been laid in the open air. In the *timbales* the macaroni were steeped in the lightest glaze and, beneath the savoury crust of flaky pastry, absorbed the flavour of the prosciutto and truffles sliced into match-like slivers.

Huge cold bass with mayonnaise followed, then stuffed turkey and avalanches of potatoes. One might expect strokes from over-eating. A fat guest, Giambalvo, nearly did pass out once: but a pailful of cold water in his face and a prudent nap in a shady room saved him. Next, all was put to rights by the arrival of one of those iced cakes at which Marsala, the cook, was a past-master. Wines, as always in sober Sicily, were of no importance. The guests expected them, of course, and liked their glasses filled to the brim, ("no collars" they would call to the footman) but in the absence of a collar to their glasses they emptied but one, at the most two.

After dusk we descended homewards.

I have spoken of excursions in the plural; in fact our only real excursion, thinking it over, was that to La Venaría. In the first years there were others, of which however I have kept only rather vague memories; though the word "vague" is not quite exact; a better phrase would be "difficult to describe". The visual impression has remained vivid in my mind but was not then linked to any word. We must have taken the carriage out to Sciacca, for instance, to lunch with the Bertolinos when I was five or six years old; but of the luncheon, the people we met, the journey, I have no memory at all. On the other hand of Sciacca itself, or rather of its promenade above the sea, such a photo-graphic, complete and precise image has remained stamped on my mind that when I returned there a couple of years ago, for the first time after more than fifty years, I was easily able to compare the scene under my eyes with the old one that had remained in my mind, and note the many similarities and the few differences.

As always memories refer particularly to memories of "light";

at Sciacca I see a very blue, almost black, sea glinting furiously beneath the midday sun, in one of those skies of high Sicilian summer which are misty with heat, a balustrade over a sheer drop to the sea, a kind of kiosk, to the left of which was a café – which is still there.

Looming skies with scudding rain-clouds, on the other hand, remind me of a small country house, Cannitello, near Catania, set on a steep hillside reached by a zig-zagging road which, I don't know why, horses had to ascend at a gallop. I see a landau with dusty blue cushions (the very fact they were blue showed that the carriage was not our own but hired), my mother sitting in a corner, panic-stricken herself but trying to reassure me, while beside us the stunted trees whirled past and vanished with the speed of wind, and the coachman's incitements mingled with whip cracks and frenzied tingling of collar-bells (no, that carriage was certainly not ours).

Of the house where we were going I retain a memory of what I can now say was its gentlemanly but poverty-stricken air; obviously I did not formulate this economic-social judgment at the time, but I can say it in all serenity now, examining the mental photograph recently retrieved from the archives of memory.

I have spoken of the people who belonged to the household at Santa Margherita; I have yet to mention the guests who came to stay for a period of days or weeks.

I have to say that these guests were few; there were no motor-cars then, or rather three or four at most in the whole of Sicily, and the ghastly state of the roads induced the owners of the *rarae aves* to use them only in towns. Santa Margherita was a long way from Palermo, then, a twelve-hour journey – and what a journey!

Amongst the guests at Santa Margherita I remember my Aunt Giulia Trigona with her daughter Clementina and the girl's nanny, a bony German woman, extremely strict and quite unlike my smiling Annas. Giovanna (now Albanese) was not yet born, and as for Uncle Romualdo, I don't know where he displayed his splendid physique and his impeccable attire.

Clementina was, and still is, a male in skirts. Blunt, resolute, truculent as she was (the very qualities which were later to turn out to her detriment), she proved a quite acceptable playmate for a little boy of six or seven. I well recall those endless pursuits, mounted on tricycles, which took place not only in the garden but indoors as well, between the entrance hall and the "Leopold drawing-room"; there and back they must have added up to a good four hundred yards.

I've already mentioned the business of our transformation into monkeys in the garden-cage; and I remember the breakfasts eaten round an iron table in the garden. I fear, though, that this latter may be a "pseudo-recollection": a photograph exists of these breakfasts in the garden, and it could very well be that I am confusing the actual recollection of the photograph with an archaic memory of childhood. This is by no means impossible, and indeed it happens all the time.

I have to say I possess no recollection of my Aunt Giulia, on this occasion; probably Clementina and I were still of an age to take our meals separately.

On the other hand I have the most vivid memory of Giovannino Cannitello. He was the proprietor of the Cannitello mansion already mentioned. Giovanni Gerbino-Xaxa, baron of Cannitello, was his full name, and he belonged to a good local family, feudatories of the Filangeri; for the Filangeri had the right, very rare and much envied, of investing with a barony a total of two of their own vassals in every generation. The Gerbinos (who had been judges of the High Court way back under the Empire) had been granted this privilege, and my grandmother even used to call him "the very first vassal among my vassals".

Giovannino Cannitello then gave me the impression of being an old man; actually he could not have been more than forty. He was very tall, very thin, very short-sighted; in spite of his spectacles, which were a *pince-nez* and had extraordinarily thick lenses, squashing down his nose with their weight, he used to walk bent in the hope of recognising at least a vague shadow of his surroundings.

A good, sensitive person, well liked and of no great intelligence, he had dedicated his life (and spent the greater part of his fortune) on trying to be "a man of fashion". And from the point of view of dress he had certainly succeeded; never have I seen a man with a wardrobe more sober, better cut, or less showy than his. He had been one of the moths drawn by the glamorous glow of the Florios, and who, after many a dizzy pirouette, dropped on to the tablecloth with burnt wings. He had been more than once to Paris with the Florios and even put up at the Ritz; and of Paris (the Paris of *boîtes*, of luxurious brothels, of high-priced ladies) he had preserved a dazzled memory which made him remarkably like the Doctor Monteleone I have mentioned before; with the difference that the engineer's memories were based on the Latin quarter and the Ecole de Médecine. They were not on very good terms, Giovannino Cannitello and Doctor Monteleone, perhaps because of their rivalry in disputing the favours of the Ville Lumière. There was a long-standing family joke about Doctor Monteleone being woken in the night because Cannitello had swallowed a litre of paraffin with a view to suicide (having been jilted by a pretty chambermaid); and he had simply turned over on his other side saying: "Shove a wick in his stomach and set it alight."

This because Giovannino Cannitello (who subsequent to the French period with Mademoiselle Sempell acquired the nickname "le grand Esco", that is, Spindleshanks) was temperamentally inclined to a vigorous pursuit of the ladies. And there is no counting the times that he made attempts on his life (by means of a circumspect use of paraffin, or brazier fumes by open window) after suffering rejection at the hands of his beloved, who generally belonged below stairs.

Poor Cannitello became almost blind and utterly destitute before he died not so many years ago (about 1932) in his house on Via Alloro, next door to the Coachmen's church. My mother, who went to visit him until the end, would return much affected by his being so bent that, when sitting in his armchair, his face was eight inches from the floor, and to talk to him she had to sit on a cushion on the very floor itself.

In the early years Alessio Cerda was also a frequent guest at Santa Margherita. Then he went blind, and although we always saw him at Palermo, he made no further appearances at Santa Margherita. There was a photograph of him dressed in his uniform as lieutenant in the *Guide*, with the soft cap, soft boots, soft gloves of our unfortunate army of 1866; all this softness was to find itself asserted at Custozza.[1] But of Alessio Cerda, a most singular personality, I shall have occasion to speak.

Another person who came once, and came indeed in one of the first motor cars, was Paolo Scaletta. I think he arrived on an off-chance: he was on his way to some Valdina properties at Menfi, not far from Santa Margherita, when his car broke down. And he came to seek our hospitality.

Many of my memories centre on Santa Margherita – agreeable and disagreeable, but all of them crucial.

---

[1] A village near Verona where in June 1866 the Austrians under the Archduke Albert routed an Italian army led by King Victor Emmanuel.

VIII

The Pink Dining-room

But I realise that I have forgotten to mention the dining-room, which was singular for various reasons; singular for existing at all; in an eighteenth-century house it was very rare, I think, to have a room set apart as a dining-room: at that time people dined in any drawing-room, changing continually, as in fact I still do now.

But there was one at Santa Margherita. Not very big, it could only hold about twenty chairs comfortably. It looked out over two balconies on to the second courtyard. Three doors gave access to it: the principal door, which led into the "picture gallery" (not the one I have already mentioned), a second which led into the "huntsmen's room", and the third giving on to the "office", whence the rope-pulley lift communicated with the kitchen below. These doors were white, Louis Seize, and had big panels with decorations in relief, gilt, of a greenish dull gold. From the ceiling hung a Murano chandelier, whose greyish glass showed up the colour of floral designs.

Prince Alessandro, who arranged this room, had thought up the idea of asking a local artist to paint on the walls pictures of himself and his family while actually eating their meals. These were large pictures on canvas, completely covering a wall from floor to ceiling with virtually lifesize figures.

One showed breakfast: the prince and princess, he in green shooting clothes, boots and wearing a hat, she in white *déshabillé* but wearing jewels, sitting at a small table intent on taking chocolate, served by a little negro slave in a turban. She was holding out a biscuit to an impatient hound, he raising towards his mouth a big blue cup decorated with flowers. Another picture represented a picnic: a number of ladies and gentlemen were sitting around a table-cloth spread in a field and covered with splendid looking pasties and grass-plaited bottles; in the background could be seen a fountain, and the trees were young and low. This, I think, must have been the actual garden of Santa Margherita just after it was planted.

A third picture, the biggest, represented a formal dinner-party with the gentlemen in very curly wigs and the ladies in full evening dress. The princess was wearing a delicious robe of silver pink *broché* silk, with a dog-collar round her neck and a great *parure* of rubies on her bosom. Footmen in full livery and cordons were entering bearing high dishes elaborately decorated.

There were another two pictures, but I can only remember the subject of one of them, for it was always facing me; this was the children's afternoon refreshment. Two little girls of ten and twelve years of age, powdered and tightly laced into their pointed bodices, sat facing a boy of about fifteen, dressed in an orange-coloured suit with black facings and carrying a rapier, and an old lady in black (certainly the governess): all were eating large ices of an odd pink colour, maybe of cinnamon, rising in sharp cones from long glass goblets.

Another of the oddities of the house was the table-centre in the dining-room. This was a large fixed silver ornament, surmounted by Neptune who threatened the guests with his trident, while beside him an Amphitrite eyed them with a hint of malice. The whole was set on a rock rising in the middle of a silver basin, surrounded by dolphins and marine monsters squirting water from their mouths through some machinery hidden in a central part of the table. It was all very gay and grand, but had the inconvenience of requiring table-cloths with a large hole cut out of the middle for Neptune. (The holes were hidden by flowers or leaves.) There were no sideboards, but four big console tables covered with pink marble, and the general tone of the room was pink, in the marble, in the princess's pink dress, in the big picture, and also in the chair coverings which were pink too, not old but of delicate hue.

For a small boy at Santa Margherita, though, adventure did not lie concealed only in unexplored apartments or in the labyrinth of the garden, but also in so many singular objects. Just think what a source of wonder that table centrepiece could be! But there was also the music-box discovered in a drawer: a big clockwork contrivance containing a cylinder set with knobs at irregular intervals, which turned on its own axis and lifted minute steel keys, producing delicate, meticulous melodies.

Near the dining-room, in another apartment, were enormous cupboards of yellow wood, the keys of which had been lost; not even Don Nofrio the administrator knew where they were, and when one said that there was no more to be said. After long hesitation the blacksmith was eventually called and the doors were opened. The cupboards contained bed linen, dozens and dozens of sheets, pillow-cases, enough for an entire hotel (there were already overwhelming quantities of these in the known cupboards); others contained blankets of real wool scattered with pepper and camphor, still others table linen, small, large or outsize damask table-cloths, all with that hole in the middle. And between one layer and another of this homely treasure were placed little tulle sacks of lavender flowers now in dust. But the most interesting cupboard was one containing writing-materials of the eighteenth century; it was a little smaller than the others, and heaped with great sheets of pure rag letter-paper, bundles of quill pens tied neatly in dozens, red and blue sealing wafers and very long sticks of sealing wax.

As can be seen, the house of Santa Margherita was a kind of eighteenth-century Pompeii, all miraculously preserved intact: a rare thing always, but almost unique in Sicily which from poverty and neglect is the most destructive of countries. I do not know what were the exact causes of this phenomenal durability: perhaps the fact that my maternal grandfather spent long years there between 1820 and 1840 in a kind of exile imposed on him by the Bourbon kings as a result of a misdemeanour on the Marine

Parade at Palermo,[1] or perhaps the passionate care which my grandmother took of it: certainly the fact of her finding in Onofrio Rotolo a unique administrator, the only one who, to my knowledge, was not a thief.

He was still alive in my time: a kind of dwarf with a long white beard, living together with an incredibly large fat wife in one of the many apartments attached to the house, with a separate entrance.

Marvels were recounted of his care and scrupulosity; how, when the house was empty, he went through it every night with lantern in hand to check that all the windows were shut and doors bolted; how he allowed only his wife to wash the precious china; how after a reception (in my grandmother's time) he checked the screws under every chair: how during the winter he spent entire days surveying squads of cleaners polishing and ordering every single object, however out-of-the-way, in that vast house. In spite of his age and anything but youthful aspect his wife was very jealous of him; and ever and again news would reach us of terrific scenes which she made due to her suspicion of his paying too much attention to the charms of some young maid-servant. I know for certain that a number of times he protested most vigorously to my mother about her over-spending; he was met, needless to say, with a deaf ear and perhaps some contumely.

His death coincided with the rapid and sudden end of this loveliest of lovely country homes. May these lines which no one will read be a homage to its unblemished memory.

---

[1] Driving his carriage stark naked.

THE PROFESSOR AND THE SIREN

A STORY

[JANUARY 1957]

In the late autumn of the year 1938, I had a bad fit of the spleen. I was living in Turin at the time, and my tart No. 1, while groping about in my pockets for an odd fifty-lire note as I slept, had also found a letter from tart No. 2, which, in spite of spelling mistakes, left no doubts about the nature of our relationship.

My awakening had been immediate and stormy. The little flat in Via Peyron echoed with vernacular tantrums; there was even an attempt to scratch my eyes out, which I only evaded by giving a slight twist to the dear girl's left wrist. This fully justified act of self-defence put an end to the scene, but to our idyll too. She flung her clothes on, thrust into her bag powder-puff, lipstick, hanky and the fifty-lire *causa mali tanti*, hissed the Torinese for "swine!" into my face thrice, and left. Never had she been so attractive as during that quarter of an hour's raging. From my window I watched her go out and move off into the morning mist, tall, slim, wrapped in reconquered poise.

Never again did I set eyes on her, as I never set eyes on a black cashmere pullover of great cost, which had the fatal quality of being styled for either male or female. All she left me, on the bed, were two of those small twisted, so-called "invisible", hairpins.

That same afternoon I had an appointment with No. 2 at a confectioner's in Piazza Carlo Felice. At the little round table in the western corner of the inner room which was "ours", I saw, not the chestnut locks of the girl who was now more than ever desirable, but the sly features of Tonino, a young brother of hers aged twelve, who had just finished gobbling down a cup of chocolate with a double portion of whipped cream. As I drew near he got up with the usual Torinese urbanity. "*Monsú*", he said, "Pinotta's not coming. She told me to give you this note. *Cerea, monsú.*" And off he went, taking with him two brioches left on the dish. In the ivory-coloured missive I was notified of summary dismissal due to my infamy and "southern dishonesty". Obviously No. 1 had traced and incited No. 2, and I was left recumbent between two stools.

In twelve hours I had lost two girls who were usefully complementary as well as a pullover I liked, and also had to pay that infernal Tonino's cake bill. My very Sicilian self-respect was humiliated: I had been made a fool of: and I decided to abandon the world and its pomps awhile.

For this period of retirement I could have found no place more suitable than the café in Via Po where I began spending every free moment alone and always went in the evening after my work on the paper. It was a kind of Hades peopled by bloodless shades of lieutenant-colonels, magistrates and professors. These insubstantial apparitions would play draughts or dominoes, immersed in a light dimmed, during the day, by arcades and clouds and at night by huge green shades on the chandeliers; no voices were ever raised lest too loud a sound disturb their tenuous woof. A most proper Limbo.

Like the creature of habit that I am, I used always to sit at the same corner table, carefully designed to offer customers a maximum of discomfort. On my left a pair of ghostly senior officers would be playing *tric-trac* with a couple of phantoms from the Court of Appeal; military and judicial dice slithered listlessly from the leather cup. On my right always sat an elderly gentleman muffled in an old overcoat with a mangy Astrakhan collar. He read foreign magazines ceaselessly, smoked Tuscan cheroots and spat a great deal: every now and again he shut up his magazines and seemed to be following some memory in the volutes of smoke. Then he would begin reading and spitting again. He had hideous, knobbly, reddish hands, with nails cut straight and not always too clean; but once when in one of those magazines his eye fell on a photograph of an archaic Greek statue, the kind with wide-set eyes and an ambiguous smile, I was surprised to see his splayed finger-tips stroke the picture with a delicacy that was almost regal. He noticed I was watching him, gave a grunt of fury and ordered another coffee.

But for a lucky accident our relations would have remained on this plane of latent hostility. I used to bring over five or six newspapers from the office, among them, once, the *Giornale di Sicilia*. Those were the years when the Ministry of so-called Popular Culture was at its fiercest, and all newspapers were identical; that number of the Palermo daily was more banal than ever and only distinguishable from a paper of Rome or Milan by its bad typography; so my reading of it was brief, and I soon dropped the sheet on the table. I had just begun to contemplate yet another incarnation of "Minculpop", when I was addressed by my neighbour: "Excuse me, sir, but might I glance at this *Giornale di Sicilia* of yours? I'm Sicilian and it's twenty years since I've seen a newspaper from home." The voice was cultivated, its accent impeccable; the old man's grey eyes looked at me with utter detachment. "Please do, of course. You know, I'm Sicilian too, and if you wish could easily bring you the newspaper here every evening." "Thank you, I don't think that's necessary; my curiosity is purely physical. If Sicily is still as it was in my day, I imagine nothing good ever happens there, as it hasn't for three thousand years."

He took a listless glance over the newspaper, refolded it, handed it back to me, and plunged into reading a pamphlet. When leaving he obviously wanted to slip off without a greeting, but I got up and introduced myself; he muttered through his teeth a name which I could not catch, but did not hold out his hand. On the threshold of the café, however, he turned round, raised his hat, and called out, "Hail, fellow-countryman!" Then he vanished beneath the arcades, leaving me dumbfounded and provoking moans of disapproval among the gambling ghosts.

I wove suitable magic spells to materialise a waiter and asked him, pointing to the empty table, "Who was that gentleman?"

"That," he replied, "is Senator Rosario La Ciura."

The name meant a lot even to my patchy journalist's culture; it was that of one of the five or six Italians who possess a reputation universal and unassailable, that of the most illustrious Hellenist of our time. Now I understood the bulky reviews and the stroking of that print; the irritability too, and the hidden refinement.

Next day at the office I searched around in that odd card-index of obituaries still "in suspense". There was a card for "La Ciura" there, decently filled in for once. It said how the great man was born at Aci-Castello (Catania) from a lower middle-class family and, through his amazing aptitude for studying Greek had, by dint of scholarships and erudite publications, attained the Chair of Greek Literature at the University of Pavia at the age of twenty-seven; he had then been called to the Chair at Turin, where he had stayed until reaching the age-limit; he had lectured at Oxford and Tübingen, and travelled extensively, for he was not only a pre-Fascist senator and Academician of the Lincei, but also doctor *"honoris causa"* of Yale, Harvard, New Delhi and Tokyo, as well, of course, as of the most illustrious universities in Europe from Uppsala to Salamanca. The list of his publications was very lengthy, and many of his works, particularly on Ionic dialects, were considered basic; proof of this was the fact that, though a foreigner, he had been charged with the Teubner edition of Hesiod, for which he had written an introduction, in Latin, of unrivalled mastery; final, major glory, he was *not* a member of the Italian Academy. What had always distinguished him from colleagues, however erudite, was his lively, almost carnal sense of classical antiquity; and this was shown in a collection of essays, in Italian, *Men and Gods*, which was considered a work not only of high erudition but of true poetry. In fact, concluded the compiler of the card, he was "an honour to the nation and a beacon to all cultures". He was seventy-five years old, and lived, not opulently but decently enough, on his pension and his senatorial emolument. He was unmarried.

There's no denying it; we Italians, elder sons (or fathers) of the Renaissance, consider the Great Humanist to be the highest form of human being. The chance of now finding myself in daily contact with the major representative of this subtle, almost magical and unremunerative branch of knowledge, flattered and perturbed me. I felt the same sensations as a young American might feel on introduction to Mr Gillette: alarm, respect, and a form of not ignoble envy.

That evening I went down to Limbo in a very different mood from that of the days before. The senator was already in his place and answered my reverential greeting with a scarcely perceptible mutter. But when he had finished reading an article and completing some notes on a little pad, he turned towards me and in strangely musical tones said, "Fellow-countryman, from your way of greeting me I see that one of these phantoms must have told you who I am. Forget it and, if you have not done so already, forget also the Aorists you studied at school. But tell me what your name is, for last night you made the usual gabbled introduction and I cannot fall back, like you, on asking others for your name, which is certainly quite unknown to anyone here."

He was talking with insolent detachment; obviously to him I was rather less than a cockroach, more like one of those specks of dust that rotate unconstructively in sunbeams. But his calm tone, his precise speech, his use of the familiar "*tu*", radiated the serenity of a Platonic dialogue.

"My name is Paolo Corbera, and I was born at Palermo, where I took a degree in law; now I am working here in the editorial offices of *La Stampa*. To reassure you, senator, I will add that in my school-leaving exam I only got five plus for Greek and have reason to think the plus was added so that I could be given a certificate at all."

He gave a half-smile. "Thank you for telling me that; better so. I detest talking to people who think themselves knowledgeable when they are ignorant, like my colleagues at the University; really all they know are the exterior forms of Greek, its oddities and deformities. The live spirit of that language which is so stupidly called 'dead' has not been revealed to them. Nothing has been revealed to them, if it comes to that. Poor wretches, anyway; how can they sense that spirit if they have never had occasion to hear real Greek?"

Pride is preferable to false modesty, yes indeed; but I felt the senator was rather over-doing it; it even occurred to me that the years might have softened a bit that exceptional brain. Those poor devils his colleagues had just the same chance of hearing ancient Greek as he had himself; none at all, that is.

He was proceeding, "Paolo ... You are lucky to be called after the only Apostle with some culture and a smattering of letters. Jerome would have been better though. The other names you Christians carry round are really too squalid; slaves' names."

I was feeling more and more disappointed; he seemed to be just an ordinary academic priest-baiter with a dash of Nietzschean Fascism added. Surely not?

He was talking on with the seductive modulations and the verve of a man who had perhaps spent a long period in silence. "Corbera ... Am I mistaken in thinking that to be one of the great Sicilian names? I remember my father used to pay a small annual ground-rent for our house at Aci-Castello to the agent of a family called Corbera di Palina or Salina, I don't remember which. He used to make a joke every time in fact, and say that if there was any sure thing in this world it was that those few lire would not end in the pockets of the "demesne" as he called them. But are you really one of those Corbera or merely a descendant of some peasant who took his master's name?"

I confessed myself to be indeed a Corbera di Salina, in fact the only surviving specimen of that family; all the splendours, all the sins, all the unexacted rents, all the unpaid bills, all the Leopard's ways in fact, were concentrated in me alone. Paradoxically the senator seemed pleased.

"Good, good. I hold old families in high regard. They possess a memory, minute it's true, but anyway greater than that of others. They are the best you people can achieve in the way of physical immortality. Get yourself married soon, Corbera, since you people have found no better way of survival than dispersing your seed in the unlikeliest places."

Definitely, I was losing patience. "You people, you people."
Who were "You people?" All the vile mob who had not the luck
to be Senator La Ciura? Had *he* attained physical immortality?
Ore wouldn't say so to look at that wrinkled face, that heavy
body ...

"Corbera di Salina," he was continuing undaunted. "You
won't be offended if I go on calling you "*tu*" as to one of those
little students of mine during their few instants of youth?"

I declared myself not only honoured but pleased, as in fact I
was. Having disposed of matters of name and protocol, we talked
of Sicily. He had not set foot on the island for twenty years, and
the last time he was "down there" (as he said in the Piedmontese
mode) he had only stayed five days, at Syracuse, to discuss with
Paolo Orsi[1] certain matters concerning the alteration of semi-
choruses in classic drama. "I remember they wanted to take me by
motor-car from Catania to Syracuse; I only accepted on learning
that at Augusta the road runs far from the sea, while the railway is
along the shore. Tell me about that island of ours; it is a lovely
land, though inhabited by donkeys. The Gods have sojourned
there, may do still in inexorable Augusts. Let us not, though,
mention those four modern temples; anyway you know nothing
about them, that I'm sure."

So we spoke about eternal Sicily, nature's Sicily; about the
scent of rosemary on the Nèbrodi hills, the taste of Melilli honey,
the waving corn seen from Etna on a windy day in May, of the
solitudes around Syracuse, the gusts of scent from orange and
lemon groves pouring over Palermo, it's said, during some
sunsets in June. We talked of the enchantment of certain summer
nights within sight of Castellamare bay, when stars are mirrored
in the sleeping sea and the spirit of anyone lying back amid the
lentisks is lost in a vortex of sky, while the body is tense and alert,
fearing the approach of demons.

After an almost total absence of fifty years the senator still kept

[1] A famous former Director of the Syracuse Museum of Classical Antiquity.

65

an extraordinarily clear memory of a few little facts. "The sea! The sea of Sicily is the most coloured, the most romantic of all I have ever seen. That will be the only thing you will not manage to ruin, apart from the cities, of course. Do they still serve those prickly sea-urchins split in half in taverns by the sea?" I reassured him, though adding that few ate them nowadays for fear of typhus. "Yet they're the best thing you have down there, those blood-red cartilages, those images of female organs, tasting of salt and sea-weed. Typhus indeed! They're dangerous as are all gifts of the sea, which grant death together with immortality. At Syracuse I demanded Orsi to produce some. What flavour! What a divine aspect! My finest memory in the last fifty years!"

I was confused and fascinated; a man like this abandoning himself to almost obscene metaphors, showing a childish greed for the, after all, mediocre delights of sea-urchins!

We went on talking for a long time, and on leaving he insisted on paying for my coffee, not without an exhibition of his peculiar boorishness ("Of course, lads of good family never have a cent in their pockets!"); and we parted friends, if one leaves out of account the fifty years dividing our ages and the thousands of light-years separating our cultures.

We went on meeting every evening, and although the smoke of my rage against humanity was now beginning to disperse I still made a point of meeting the senator unfailingly in the Infernal regions of Via Po. Not that we chatted much: he would go on reading and taking notes and only addressed me now and again, but when he did it was always a harmonious flow of pride and insolence, sprinkled with varied allusions, veined with incomprehensible poetry.

He went on spitting too, and eventually I noticed that he did so only while reading. I think he must have acquired a certain affection for me too, but I am under no illusions about that; if he did have any, it was not what one of "us people" (to use the Senator's term) might feel for a human being, but more like an old spinster's affection for her pet canary, of whose fatuity and incomprehension she is aware but whose existence permits her to express aloud regrets in which the little creature has no part; on the other hand, if it were not there, she would feel ill-at-ease. I began noticing, in fact, that whenever I was late the old man's haughty eyes were fixed on the entrance door.

It took nearly a month for us to move on from his always highly original but general comments to the indiscretions which alone make conversations between friends differ from those between mere acquaintances. I myself took the initiative. That frequent spitting of his worried me (as it worried the custodians of the Hades, who had eventually put a dark copper spittoon beside his chair), and one evening I was bold enough to ask him why he did not go to a doctor about his chronic catarrh. I asked the question unthinkingly, at once regretted having risked it, and waited for the senatorial anger to bring the stucco ceiling down on my head. Instead of which the well-modulated voice replied placidly; "But, my dear Corbera, I have no catarrh. A keen observer like yourself should have noticed that I never cough before I spit. My spitting is no sign of illness, but rather of mental health. I spit from disgust at the nonsense I am reading. If you care to examine that utensil there" (and he pointed at the spittoon) "you would realise that it contains very little saliva and no trace of mucus. My spits are symbolic and of high cultural content; if you don't like 'em then go back to your native drawing-rooms, where there's no spitting only because no one will ever admit themselves to be nauseated by anything."

The gross insolence of this was attenuated by a faraway look, yet even so I felt like getting up and leaving him there and then; luckily I had time to reflect that I had only my own rashness to blame. I stayed, and at once the impassive senator counter-attacked; "Now *you* tell *me* why you frequent this ghost-filled and, as you say, catarrh-ridden Erebus, this geometric site of failed lives? In Turin there's no lack of these creatures whom to you people seem so desirable. A trip to that hotel by the castle, to Rivoli or the baths at Moncalieri, and your prurient urges would soon find an object." I burst into laugher at hearing from so learned a mouth such exact information on the pleasure haunts of

Turin. "But how d'you come to know these addresses, senator?" "I know them, Corbera, I know them. That is the one thing, and the one thing only, that one does learn from frequenting senates, both academic and political. But please do me the favour of being convinced that the sordid pleasures of you people have never been Rosario La Ciura's." That, one felt, was true; the senator's bearing and words bore the unequivocal sign (as we used to say in 1938) of a sexual reserve quite unconnected with age.

"The truth, senator, is that I began coming here as a temporary refuge from the world. I've had trouble with two of the sort of girls you so justly stigmatise."

His reply was sharp and frank. "Cuckoldry, eh, Corbera? Or pox?"

"Neither: worse, desertion." And I told him about the ridiculous events of two months before. My tone was facetious, for the ulcer on my self-respect had healed. Any man other than this devilish Hellenist would have either jeered at me or, more rarely, sympathised. But the alarming old man did neither: he waxed indignant. "You see what happens, Corbera, as a result of coupling with the squalid and the diseased? I would say the same to those two sluts about you if I ever had the misfortune to meet them."

"Disease, senator? They were both in splendid health; you should have seen the amount they ate at the *Specchi*; and not in the least squalid; superb creatures, both of them, and elegant too." The senator hissed out one of his contemptuous spits. "Diseased, I said, diseased: in fifty, sixty years, maybe long before, they'll crack up; so from now on they're sick. And squalid: elegant indeed, with their trashy jewellery, stolen pullovers, and airs and graces taken from the films! Splendour indeed, fishing about for greasy bank-notes in their lover's pocket instead of presenting him, as others do, with rose-pink pearls and branches of coral! That's just what happens to people who go with these slapped-up sluts. And were you not at all disgusted, they as much as you, you as much as they, at cuddling yours and their future carcases between stinking sheets?" I was stupid enough to reply, "but the sheets were always perfectly clean, senator!" He became furious. "What have sheets to do with it? The inevitable stink of corpses was your own. I repeat, how can you wallow about with people of their, of your sort?" I, who had just been eyeing one of Ventura's delicious *cousettes*, took offence. "Well, one can't go to bed only with Serene Highnesses!" "Who mentioned 'Serene Highnesses'? They're as much charnel-house material as the others. But these are matters you cannot understand, young man, and I'm wrong to mention them. You and your little girl-friends are fated to sink deeper and deeper into the pestilential mire of your slimy pleasures. Those who really know are so few."

He began to smile with eyes turned towards the ceiling: his face had a rapt expression: then he held out his hand to me and left.

He did not appear again for three days; on the fourth I had a telephone-call at the newspaper-office. "Is that *Monsù* Corbera? This is Bettina, housekeeper to *Signour* Senator La Ciura. He says to tell you that he's had a bad cold, that he's better now, and that he'd like to see you tonight after dinner. Come to 18, Via Bertola at nine; second floor." The line was suddenly cut, and I could not ring back.

Number 18 Via Bertola was a dilapidated old building, but the senator's apartment was large and well-kept, due, presumably, to the persistent care of Bettina. The parade of books began from the entrance hall, the sort of modest-looking cheaply bound volumes of every living library. There were thousands in the three rooms I crossed. In the fourth sat the senator wrapped in an ample camel-hair dressing-gown, the finest and softest I had ever seen. Later I learnt this was not camel-hair but rare llama wool, a gift from the Academic Senate of Lima. Though the senator pointedly did not rise on my entry, he greeted me most cordially; he felt better, quite well in fact, and expected to be back in circulation as soon as the wave of cold then over Turin grew milder. He offered me some resinated Cypriot wine, a gift from the Italian Institute of Athens, some foul pink "lucums" from the Archaeological Mission of Ankara, and sensible Torinese cakes acquired by the provident Bettina. He was in such good humour that he actually smiled twice with his whole mouth and even reached the point of apologising for his own outbursts in our Hades. "I know, Corbera, I have been excessive in my terms, though believe me, moderate in my concepts. Don't give it another thought." I was in fact not thinking of it, but feeling full of respect for this old man whom I suspected of being very unhappy in spite of his triumphant career. He was devouring those abominable "lucums". "Sweets, Corbera, should be sweet and no more. If they have any other flavour they're like perverse kisses."

He was giving big morsels to Aeacus, a large boxer dog which had entered the room. "This creature, Corbera, in spite of his ugliness is more like the Immortals, to one who can understand such things, than any of your little bitches."

He refused to show me his library. "All classics that could have no interest for one like you, who are morally failed in Greek." But he did take me round the room we were in, which turned out to be his study. It contained few books, among them the plays of Tirso de Molina, Lamotte-Fouqué's *L'Undine*, Giraudoux's play of the same name, and, to my surprise, the works of H. G. Wells. But in compensation the walls were hung with huge photographs, life-size, of archaic Greek statues; and not the usual photographs we can all lay hands on, but superb specimens, obviously demanded with authority and despatched with devotion from museums all over the world. There they all were, those magnificent creatures, the "Rider" in the Louvre, the "Seated Goddess" from Taranto now in Berlin, the "Warrior" of Delphi, the "Korè" of the Acropolis, the "Apollo" of Piombino, the "Lapithae Woman" and the "Phoebus" at Olympia, the famous "Charioteer" . . . The room was alight with their ecstatic yet ironic smiles, exalted by the relaxed arrogance of their bearing. "You see, Corbera; these, yes; tarts, no."

On the mantelshelf were ancient amphorae and vases; Odysseus tied to the ship's mast, the Sirens crashing from a high precipice on to rocks in expiation for letting their prey escape. "All nonsense that, Corbera, petty bourgeois poets' tales. No one ever escapes the Sirens, and even if someone did they would never have died for so little. How could they have died, anyway?"

On a small table, in a modest frame, stood an old faded photograph: a youth of about twenty, almost naked, with unruly curls and a confident look on features of rare beauty. Perplexed, I paused an instant, thinking I had understood. Not at all. "And this, fellow-countryman, this was and is and shall be" (he accentuated strongly) "Rosario La Ciura."

The poor senator in a dressing-gown had been a young god.

Then we spoke of other things, and before I left he showed me a letter in French from the Rector of the University of Coimbra inviting him to join the Committee of Honour for a congress of Greek studies which was to take place in Portugal that May. "I'm very pleased about it; I'll embark at Genoa on the *Rex* with the French, Swiss and German congress members. Like Odysseus I shall stop my ears to avoid hearing the nonsense of those maimed creatures. But there will be lovely days of navigation: sun, blue, smell of sea."

On our way out we passed the bookcase holding the works of Wells, and I dared to express my surprise at finding them there. "You're right, Corbera, they're a horror. And among them there's a short novel that would make me want to spit for a month on end if I re-read it; and you wouldn't like that, would you, you drawing-room lapdog?"

After this visit of mine our relations became definitely cordial, on my side at least. I made elaborate preparations for some really fresh sea-urchins to be sent up from Genoa. When told they would arrive next day I laid in some Etna wine and peasant bread, then timidly invited the senator to visit my little abode. I went to fetch him in my Fiat *Balilla*, and drove him all the way out to Via Peyron, which is at the back of beyond. In the motor-car he showed some alarm and utter distrust in my driving capacities. "I know you now, Corbera; if we have the misfortune to meet one of those skirted monstrosities of yours you're quite capable of turning right round, then we'll both go and crack our noses on a kerb." We met no noteworthy abortions in skirts and arrived intact.

For the first time since I had known him I saw the senator laugh; this was on entering my bedroom. "So this is the theatre of your grubby ruttings, is it, Corbera!" He examined my few books. "Good, good. Maybe you're less ignorant than you seem. This man here," he added, taking up my Shakespeare, "this man here did understand something. *'A sea change into something rich and strange. What potions have I drunk of Siren tears?'*"

When good Signora Carmagnola entered the sitting-room with a tray of sea-urchins, lemons and the rest, the senator was in ecstasies. "What? You thought of this, did you? How can you know that these are what I yearn for most?"

"You're quite safe in eating them, senator, they were in the sea on the Riviera only this morning."

"Yes, of course, always the same, you people, slaves to decay and putrescence, always with ears strained for the shuffling steps of Death. Poor devils! Thank you, Corbera, you've been a good *famulus*. A pity they're not from that sea 'down there', these sea-urchins, that they aren't wrapped in our own seaweed; their prickles have certainly never made any divine blood flow. You've done all you possibly could, of course, but these are almost wild sea-urchins that were dozing in the chilly rocks of Nervi or Arenzano." Obviously he was one of those Sicilians who consider the Ligurian Riviera (a tropical region to the Milanese) a kind of Iceland. The sea-urchins, split, exhibited their wounded, blood-red, strangely partitioned flesh. I had never noticed before, but now, after the senator's bizarre comparisons, they really did seem to me like a cross-section of some delicate female organ. He was eating them avidly but without gaiety, quiet, almost absorbed. He would squeeze no lemon over them. "You people are always coupling flavours! A sea-urchin must also taste of lemon, sugar of chocolate, love of paradise!"

When he had finished he took a sip of wine, and closed his eyes. Soon after I noticed two tears slide from under his withered lids. He got up, moved over to the window, surreptitiously wiped his eyes. Then he turned. "Have you ever been to Augusta, Corbera?"

I had been there three months as a recruit; during time off two or three of us used to take out a boat and meander around the transparent waters of the bays. After my reply he was silent; then said in a tone of irritation; "And did you milk-sops ever visit that little inner bay beyond Punta Izzo, behind the hill overlooking the salt pans?"

"Indeed we did; it's the loveliest spot in Sicily, fortunately so far undiscovered by the Young Fascists' organisations. A wild bit of coast, isn't it, senator? Utterly deserted, not a house in sight; the sea is peacock-coloured; and right opposite, beyond the iridescent waves, Etna. From nowhere else as from there is it so lovely, so calm, masterful, truly divine. It is one of those places in which one sees an eternal aspect of that island of ours which so idiotically turned its back on its vocation, that of serving as pasturage for the herds of the sun."

The senator was silent. Then; "You're a good lad, Corbera; if you were not so ignorant one could have made something of you."

He came up to me, kissed me on the forehead. "Now go and fetch that little coffee-grinder of yours. I want to go home."

During the following weeks we went on meeting as usual. Now we would take nocturnal walks, usually along Via Po and across the martial Piazza Vittorio in order to gaze at the rushing river and the hill, where they introduced a touch of fantasy into the geometric pattern of the city. It was the beginning of spring, that touching season of threatened youth; first lilacs were sprouting on banks, the more eager haven-less couples defying damp grass. "Down in Sicily the sun is already burning, the seaweed aflower; fish are surfacing on moonlight nights, their flashing bodies glimpsed amid luminous spray. And here we stand facing this insipid and deserted stream, these great barracks that look like rows of soldiers or friars, and hear the moaning of these couplings of the dying."

But he cheered at the thought of the sea-journey he would soon be taking to Lisbon; departure was close now. "It will be pleasant; you should come too; a pity, though, that there's no group for people lacking in Greek; you could talk Italian to me, but if you didn't show Zuckmayer or Van der Voos a knowledge of the optatives of all irregular Greek verbs you'd be out. Though maybe you are more conscious of Greek reality than they; not by culture, of course, but by animal instinct."

Two days before he left for Genoa he told me he would not be coming to the café next day but would be expecting me at his home at nine that night.

The ceremonial was the same as on my other visit: the pictures of the gods of three thousand years ago radiated youth as a stove radiates heat; the faded photograph of the young god of fifty years before seemed dismayed to look at his own metamorphosis, white-haired and slumped in an armchair.

When the Cypriot wine was drunk the senator called for Bettina and told her she could go to bed. "I will see Signor Corbera out myself when he goes. Now, Corbera, if I've brought you here to-night at the risk of disarranging one of your fornications at Rivoli, it's because I need you. I leave to-morrow, and at my age when one goes away one never knows if it won't be a matter of staying afar for ever; particularly on a journey by sea. You know, really I'm quite fond of you; your simplicity touches me, the obvious machinations of your vital forces amuse me; then I have an idea that you, as happens with a few Sicilians of the better kind, have succeeded in achieving a synthesis between your senses and your reason. So you deserve not to be left dry-mouthed, without my explaining to you the reason for some of my oddities, of some of the phrases I have uttered in front of you and which you must have thought worthy of a madman."

I protested feebly. "Much of what you said I've not understood; but I've always attributed my incomprehension to the inadequacy of my own mind, never to an aberration of yours."

"No matter, Corbera, it's all the same to me. All us old men

74

seem mad to you young ones, yet often it's the other way round. To explain myself, though, I shall have to describe my adventure to you, which I seldom do. It happened when I was that young gentleman there," and he pointed to the photograph of himself. "We must go back to 1887, a time which must seem prehistoric to you, but is not so to me."

He moved from his own chair behind the desk and came to sit on the sofa beside me. "Excuse me, you know, but later on I'll have to speak in a low voice. Important words can't be yelled; the scream of love or hate is only heard in melodrama or among the most uncivilised, which comes to the same thing. Anyway, in 1887 I was twenty-four years old; my aspect was that of the photograph; I already had a degree in classics, and published two small studies on Ionic dialects which had made some stir at my university; and for the last year I'd been preparing to compete for a Chair at Pavia University. To say the truth, never, before that year or since, had I or have I touched a woman."

I was sure that my face remained marmoreally impassive, but I was deceived. "That wink of yours is very ill-mannered, Corbera. What I'm saying is the truth; truth and also boast. I know that we males of Catania are generally thought capable of making our very wetnurses pregnant, which may well be true. Not in my case, though. When one spends night and day in the company of gods and demi-gods, as I was doing at the time, one is left with little desire to climb the stairs of San Berillio brothels. Also I was held back by religious scruples at the time. Corbera, you really must learn to control your eyelashes: they betray you again and again. Yes. Religious scruples, I said. I also said 'at the time'. Now I no longer have them, but that's been no use to me in this matter.

"You, my little Corbera, who probably got your job on the newspaper due to a note from some Fascist boss, can have no idea of the preparation needed to compete for a university chair in Greek literature. It means two years of slogging away to the verge of madness. The language, luckily, I knew well enough already, as well as I do now; and I don't wish to boast but ... The rest though; the Alexandrian and Byzantine variants of texts, the quotations, always inaccurate, perpetrated by Latin authors, the innumerable connections between literature and mythology, history, philosophy, science! I repeat, it's enough to drive anyone mad. So there I was studying away and, on top of that, cramming boys who'd failed their school exams in order to pay my keep in town. I was living on more or less nothing but black olives and coffee. Then to crown it all came that appalling summer of 1887, which was one of the truly hellish ones that happen down there now and again. At night Etna would vomit the sun's fire that it had stored during fifteen hours of daylight; touching a balcony-rail at midday meant a rush to a First Aid post; the lava paving-stones seemed on the point of returning to their fluid state; and almost every day the scirocco flapped its slimy bats' wings in one's face. I was all in. A friend saved me: he met me as I was wandering deranged through the streets, stuttering Greek verses which I no longer understood. My appearance alarmed him. 'Listen, Rosario, if you stay on here you'll go off your head and that will be the end of your chair. I'm off to Switzerland' (the boy had money) 'but I've a three-roomed hut at Augusta twenty yards from the sea, way out of town. Pack your bag, take your books and go and spend the whole summer there. Call at my home in an hour's time and I'll give you the key. You'll see, it's quite different there. Ask at the station where the Casino Carobene is, everyone knows it. But do leave, leave to-night.'

"I took his advice and left that night; next morning, instead of being greeted at dawn by lavatory pipes across a courtyard I woke up facing a pure stretch of sea with, in the background, an Etna no longer ruthless, wrapped in morning mist. The port was utterly deserted, as you tell me it still is, and uniquely lovely. All that the shabby rooms of the little house contained were the couch on which I spent the night, a table and three chairs; also a few earthenware pots and an old lamp in the kitchen. Behind the house was a fig-tree and a well. Paradise. I went into town, traced the peasant who looked after the Carobene's patch of land, and arranged for him to bring me bread, spaghetti, a few vegetables and some petroleum every two or three days. Oil I had, our own, sent by my poor mother down to Catania. I hired a small boat which a fisherman brought me over every afternoon together with a lobster-pot and a few fishing-hooks. There I made up my mind to stay at least two months.

"Carobene was right: it really was quite different. The heat was violent at Augusta too, but it no longer reverberated from every wall, no longer produced utter prostration but a kind of suppressed euphoria; the sun put off its executioner's scowl and contented itself with the role of splendid if brutal donor of energy, as well as of a magic jeweller who set mobile diamonds in every faintest ripple of sea. Study had ceased to be an effort; to the gentle rocking of the boat in which I spent long hours each book became, instead of an obstacle, a key opening up a world, one of whose most entrancing aspects I already had beneath my eyes. Often I found myself declaiming verses of poets aloud, and the names of those forgotten gods, ignored by most, again skimmed the surface of that sea which once at their name alone had risen in tumult or relapsed into a lull.

"My isolation was complete, interrupted only by visits from the peasant who brought me a few provisions every three or four days. He only stayed five minutes, because the sight of my elated carefree state must have made him think me on the verge of dangerous madness. And, in truth, sun, solitude, nights spent beneath rotating stars, silence, sparse feeding, study of remote subjects, did weave a kind of spell around me which predisposed a mood for prodigy.

"This was fulfilled at six o'clock on the morning of the fifth of August. I had just awoken and got straight into the boat; a few strokes of the oars had borne me far from the pebbles on the beach, and I had stopped under a large rock whose shadow would protect me from the sun, already climbing in swollen ferment and turning to gold and blue the candour of the dawn sea. I was declaiming away when I suddenly felt the edge of the boat lower, to the right, behind me, as if someone had seized it to climb on board. I turned and saw her: a smooth sixteen-year-old face

77

emerging from the sea, two small hands gripping the gunwale. The girl smiled, a slight fold drawing aside her pale lips and showing a glimpse of sharp little white teeth like a dog's. But it was not in the least like one of those smiles you people give, which are always debased by an accessory expression, of benevolence or irony, pity, cruelty or the like; this expressed nothing but itself, that is an almost animal joy, an almost divine delight in existence. This smile was the first of the spells cast upon me, revealing paradises of forgotten serenity. From rumpled sun-coloured hair the seawater flowed over green widely open eyes down features of childlike purity.

"Our captious reason, however predisposed, rears up before a prodigy, and when faced with one falls back on memories of the obvious; I tried, as anyone else would, to persuade myself I had met a girl out bathing, and moved carefully over above her, bent down and held out my hands to help her in. But she with astounding vigour emerged straight from the sea as far as the waist and put her arms round my neck, enwrapping me in a scent I had never smelt before, then let herself slither into the boat: beneath her groin, beneath her gluteal muscles, her body was that of a fish, covered in minute scales of blue and mother-of-pearl and ending in a forked tail which was slowly beating the bottom of the boat. She was a Siren.

"She lay on her back with head resting on crossed hands, showing with serene immodesty a delicate down under her armpits, drawn-apart breasts, perfectly shaped loins; from her arose what I have wrongly called a scent but was more a magic smell of sea, of youthful voluptuousness. We were in shade, but twenty yards away the beach lay abandoned to the sun and quivering with sensuality. My reaction was ill-hidden by my almost utter nudity.

"She spoke: and so after her smile and her smell I was submerged by the third and greatest of charms, that of voice. It was slightly guttural, veiled, reverberating with innumerable harmonies; behind the words could be sensed the lazy surf of summer seas, last spray rustling on a beach, winds passing on lunar waves. The song of the Sirens does not exist, Corbera: the music from which there is no escaping is that of their voices.

"She was speaking in Greek and I had great difficulty in understanding her: 'I heard you talking to yourself in a language similar to my own; I like you; take me. I am Lighea, daughter of Calliope. Don't believe in the tales invented about us; we kill none, we only love.'

"Bent over her, I rowed, gazing into her laughing eyes. We reached the shore; I took that aromatic body in my arms and we passed from glare to deep shade; she was already bringing to my mouth that flavour of pleasure which compared to your earthly kisses is like wine to tap-water."

The senator was describing his adventure in a low voice. I, who in my heart had always considered my own varied sexual experiences as far superior to what I had thought of as his mediocre ones and who had stupidly felt that this diminished the distance between us, was humiliated; even in love I found myself submerged in abysmal depths below him. Never for an instant did I suspect him to be telling me lies, and the greatest sceptic, had he been present, would have sensed the utter truth in the old man's tone.

"So those three weeks began. It is not proper, it would anyway not be charitable towards you, to enter into details. Suffice it to say that in those embraces I enjoyed both the highest forms of spiritual pleasure and that elementary one, quite without any social connotations, felt by our lonely shepherds on the hills when they couple with their own goats; if the comparison disgusts you that is because you are incapable of making the necessary transposition from the bestial to the superhuman plane, in my case superimposed on each other.

"Think again of what Balzac dared not express in his *Une passion dans le désert*. Those immortal limbs of hers emanated such a life-force that every loss of energy was at once replenished, in fact increased. During those days, Corbera, I loved as much as a hundred of your Don Juans put together in their whole lives. And what love! Immune from convents or crimes, from

79

Commander's rages and Leporello's trivialities, away from the pretensions of the heart, from the false sighs and sham deliquescence which inevitably blot your wretched kisses. A Leporello did, actually, disturb us that first day; it was the only time: towards ten o'clock I heard the peasant's heavy boots on the path leading to the sea. Scarcely had I time to draw a sheet over Lighea's unusual figure than he was already at the door: her head, neck, and arms which were uncovered, made Leporello think it was some ordinary little romp and this induced a sudden respect in him; he stayed for even less time than usual and as he went off winked his left eye and with thumb and forefinger of his right hand rolled and shut made a gesture of twiddling an imaginary moustache at the corner of his mouth; then he clambered off up the path.

"I have spoken of our spending twenty days together; but I would not like you to think that during those three weeks she and I lived as 'man and wife', as the expression goes, sharing bed, food and occupations. Lighea was very often away; without any previous hint she would plunge into the sea and vanish, sometimes for many hours. When she returned, usually early in the morning, she would either meet me in the boat, or, if I was still indoors, slither on her back over the pebbles, half in and half out of the water, pushing herself along by the arms and calling for me to help her up the slope. 'Sasà', she used to call me, as I had told her that was the diminutive of my name. In this action, hampered by that very part of her body which made her so agile in the sea, she had the pitiful aspect of a wounded animal, an aspect which the laughter in her eyes cancelled at once.

"She ate only what was alive: often I saw her emerge from the sea, her delicate torso gleaming in the sun, tearing in her teeth a silvery fish that was still quivering; the blood flowed in lines on her chin, and after a few bites the mangled cod-fish or dory would be flung over her shoulder and sink into the water, tainting it with red, while she let out childish cries as she cleaned her teeth with her tongue. Once I gave her some wine; she was incapable of drinking from a glass and I had to pour some into her minute and faintly greenish palm, from which she drank by lapping it up with her tongue like a dog, while surprise spread in her eyes at that unknown flavour. She said it was good, but always refused it afterwards. Occasionally she would come ashore with hands full of oysters and mussels, and while I laboured to open the shell with a knife she would crack them with a stone and suck in the palpitating mollusc together with shreds of shell which did not bother her.

"As I told you, Corbera, she was a beast but at the same instant also an Immortal, and it is a pity that no speech can express this synthesis continually, with such utter simplicity, as she expressed it in her own body. Not only did she show a joyousness and delicacy in the carnal act quite the opposite of dreary animal lust, but her talk had a potent immediacy which I have found since only in a few great poets. Not for nothing is she the daughter of Calliope: ignorant of all culture, unaware of all wisdom, contemptuous of any moral inhibitions, she belonged, even so, to the fountainhead of all culture, of all wisdom, of all ethics, and could express this primitive superiority of hers in terms of rugged beauty. 'I am everything because I am simply the current of life, with its detail eliminated; I am immortal because in me every death meets, from that of the fish just now to that of Zeus, and conjoined in me they turn again into a life that is no longer individual and determined but Pan's and so free.' Then she would say; 'You are young and handsome; follow me now into the sea and you will avoid sorrow and old age; come to my dwelling beneath the high mountains of dark motionless waters where all is silence and quiet, so infused that who possesses it does not even notice it. I have loved you; and remember that when you are tired, when you can drag on no longer, you have only to lean over the sea and call me; I will always be there because I am everywhere, and your thirst for sleep will be assuaged.'

"She told me about her existence beneath the sea, about bearded Tritons and translucent caverns, but she said that those too were unreal visions and that the truth lay much deeper, in the blind mute palace of formless waters, eternal, without a gleam, without a whisper.

"Once she told me she would be away a long while, till the evening of the next day. 'I must go a long way off, to where I know I shall find a gift for you.'

"She returned with a superb branch of lilac coral encrusted with sea-shells and barnacles. For years I used to keep this in a drawer and kiss every night the places on where I remembered to have rested the fingers of the Indifferent, that is of the Beneficent One. Then one day Maria, a housekeeper of mine before Bettina, stole it to give a ponce. I found it later at a goldsmith's on the Ponte Vecchio, desecrated, cleaned and polished so that it was almost unrecognisable. I bought it back and that night flung it into the Arno: it had passed through too many hands.

"She also spoke of the considerable number of human lovers she had had during that millenial adolescence of hers; fishermen and sailors; Greek, Sicilian, Arab, Capresi; one or two ship-wrecked mariners too, adrift on rotting rafts, to whom she had appeared for a second, in the lightning flashes of a storm, to change their deathrattle into ecstasy. 'All have followed up my invitation and come to me again, some at once, others after the passage of what for them was a long time. There was only one I never saw again; a fine big lad with very white skin and red hair with whom I coupled on a distant beach over where our sea joins the great Ocean; he smelt of something even stronger than that wine you gave me the other day. I think he never appeared not because I did not make him happy but because he was so drunk when we met that he did not understand a thing; probably I seemed like one of his usual fisher-girls.'

"Those weeks of high summer sped by as fast as a single morning; when they were over I realised that actually I had lived for centuries. That lascivious girl, that cruel wild beast, had also been a Wise Mother who by her mere presence had uprooted faiths, dissipated metaphysics. With those fragile often blood-covered fingers she had shown me the way towards true eternal repose, and also towards an asceticism derived not from

82

renunciation but from an incapacity to accept other inferior pleasures. Certainly I shall not be the second man to disobey her call, I will not refuse that kind of pagan Grace that has been conceded me.

"Due to its very violence, that summer was short. Just after the 20th of August the first timid clouds began collecting and a few isolated drops of rain fell, tepid as blood. The nights were an enfolding chain of slow, mute lightning flashes, following each other on the distant horizon like the cogitations of a god. In the mornings the dove-coloured sea would moan like a turtle-dove with arcane restlessness, and in the evenings crinkle without any perceptible breeze in gradations of smoke-grey, steel-grey, pearl-grey, all gentle colours more tender than the former splendour. Far away wisps of mist grazed the waters: maybe on the coasts of Greece it was already raining. Lighea's mood also changed in colour from splendour to tender grey. She was silent more often, spent hours stretched on a rock gazing at a horizon no longer motionless, seldom went away. 'I want to stay on with you; if I leave the shore now my companions of the sea will keep me back. Do you hear them? They're calling me.' Sometimes I did seem to hear a different, lower note amid the screech of sea-gulls, to glimpse unruly flashes from rock to rock. 'They are sounding their shells, calling Lighea for the storm festival!'

"This hit us at dawn on the 26th. From the rock we saw the wind sweep closer, fling the distant waters into confusion, as near us swelled vast and leaden billows. Soon the broadside reached us, whistled in our ears, bent the dried-up rosemary bushes. The sea below us did not break; along came the first white-crowned wave. 'Good-bye, Sasà. You won't forget!' The roller crashed on our rock, the Siren flung herself into iridescent surf; I did not see her drop; she seemed to dissolve into the spray."

The senator left next morning; I went to the station to see him off. He was grumpy and acid as always, but just when the train began to move his fingers reached out of the little window and grazed my head.

Next day, at dawn, came a telephone call to the newspaper from Genoa; during the night Senator La Ciura had fallen into the sea from the deck of the *Rex* as it was steaming towards Naples, and although life-boats had been launched at once the body had not been found.

A week later his will was opened; the money in the bank and his furniture went to Bettina; the library was left to the University of Catania; by a codicil of recent date I was left the Greek vase with the Siren figures and a large photograph of the Korè on the Acropolis.

Both objects I sent down to my home in Palermo. Then came the war, and while I was in Marmarica rationed to half a litre of water a day "Liberators" destroyed my home; on my return I found the photograph had been cut into strips to serve as torches for night-looters; the bowl was smashed; in the largest fragment can be seen the feet of Ulysses tied to his ship's mast. I still keep it. The books were stored in cellars at the University, but as there is no money for shelves they are slowly rotting away.

THE BLIND KITTENS

THE FIRST CHAPTER OF AN
UNCOMPLETED NOVEL
[MARCH 1957]

The plan of the Ibba property, on a scale of 1 to 5,000, covered a strip of oiled paper six foot long and two and a half feet wide. Not that everything shown on the map belonged to the family: there was, first of all, to the south a narrow strip of sea belonging to no one on a coast line fringed with tunny fisheries; to the north were inhospitable mountains on which the Ibbas had never wanted to lay their hands; and, amid the mass of lemon-yellow indicating various family properties, were a number of fair-sized white blobs: lands that never came on the market because the owners were rich: lands that had been offered but refused because they were of too low a quality, lands desired but in the hands of people who were still, at it were, undercooked, not yet fit for mastication. There were also a very few pieces of land which had been yellow and turned white again when resold to acquire other, better land during bad years when ready money was scarce. In spite of these splodges (all marginal), the main mass of yellow was imposing: from an oval-shaped inner nucleus round Gibilmonte a wide claw extended eastwards, gradually narrowed, then broadening again pushed out two tentacles, one towards the sea, which it reached for a small stretch, the other northwards to the lower slopes of precipitous and sterile hills. Westwards expansion was even bigger: these were ex-church lands in which advance had been as fast as a knife through lard: the hamlets of S. Giacinto and S. Narciso had been occupied and overrun by the flying columns of the Expropriation Acts; a defensive line on the river Favarotta had just collapsed after holding out a long time; and that day, the 14th September 1901, a bridgehead had been established on the far side of the river by the purchase of Pispisa, a small but succulent estate on the right bank.

The newly bought property had not yet been coloured in yellow on the plan, but Chinese ink and a thin brush were already waiting on a desk for the hand of Calcedonio, the only person in the house who knew how to make proper use of them. Don Batassano Ibba himself, head of the family and near-baron, had tried his hand ten years before when Scíddico had been expropriated, but with distressing results: a yellow tide had spread over the whole map and a heap of money had to be spent on having a new one done. The little bottle of ink, though, was still the same. So this time Don Batassano did not risk trying his hand and merely stared with his brazen peasant's eyes at the place to be coloured, thinking that the Ibba lands would show up now even on a map of all Sicily, flea size in the vastness of the island, of course, but still clearly visible.

Don Batassano was satisfied but also irritated, two states of mind often co-existing in him. That man Ferrara, the Prince of Salina's agent who had arrived this morning to arrange the deed of sale, had quibbled right up to the very moment of signature and even after! And he'd wanted the money paid in eighty of the Bank of Sicily's big pink notes, instead of the letters of credit prepared for him; he, Don Batassano, had had to climb up stairs and draw the cash from a secret drawer in his own desk, a most risky operation because Mariannina and Totò might be around at that hour. True, the agent had let himself be bamboozled about a tithe of eighty lire a year to the Church Fund, for which he had agreed to take off a thousand six hundred lire from the capital value, while Don Batassano (and the notary too) knew that it had already been compounded nine years before by another of the Salinas' agents. This had no effect though; any opposition, however slight, to his own will, particularly in regard to money, exasperated him; "They're forced to sell with the water at their chins, but still fuss about the difference between banknotes and letters of credit!"

It was only four o'clock and there were five hours to go before supper. Don Batassano opened the window on to a narrow yard. The sultry September air, cooked, recooked, resteeped, infused the darkened room. Down below an old man with heavy moustaches was spreading bird-lime on bamboo rods; he was preparing his young master's pastime. "Giacomino, saddle the horses, mine and yours. I'm coming down."

He wanted to go and see the damage to a water trough at Scíddico: some urchins had smashed one side of a basin, so he had been told that morning; the leak had been stopped temporarily with rubble and that mixture of mud and straw always to be found beside horse-troughs; but Tano, the tenant at Scíddico, had asked for proper repairs at once. More bother, more expense; and if he did not go and see in person the workmen would put in an exorbitant bill. He assured himself that his holster with its heavy Smith & Wesson was hanging from his belt, (he was so used to having it always on him that he no longer noticed it), and went down some slate steps into the yard. The keeper was just saddling the horses; he mounted his from three brick steps put against a wall for that purpose, took a switch held out by a boy, waited until Giacomino (without help from his master's mounting steps) was in the saddle. The keeper's son flung open fortified gates, summer afternoon light flooded the yard, and Don Batassano Ibba issued with his bodyguard into the main street of Gibilmonte.

The two rode along almost side by side, Giacomino's horse only half a head behind his master's: the keeper's "two-shooters" exhibited their iron butts, their polished barrels to right and left of the saddle. The animals' hooves clattered irregularly over the cobbles of narrow alleys. Women sitting weaving in front of their doors gave no greeting. "Life!" cried Giacomino every now and again as some small completely naked urchin was about to roll between the horses' hooves; dangling on a chair, his head against a wall of the church, the archpriest pretended to be asleep: anyway the living was not in the gift of this rich Ibba here but of the poor absentee Santapau. Only the sergeant of Carabinieri, in shirt-sleeves at a balcony of the barracks, leant over with a greeting. They left the village, climbed the track leading to the fork. A great deal of water had been lost during the night, and it had formed a big stagnant pond all around: mixed with mud, chaff, manure, cows' urine, it exhaled a sharp stink of ammonia. But the temporary repairs had done their job; water was no longer flowing between cracks in the stone basin, only trickling, and the thin stream issuing in spurts from a rusty tube was enough to make up the loss. Don Batassano was so pleased at what had been done costing nothing that he overlooked the repair's temporary nature. "What nonsense Tano talked! The basin's in fine condition! It doesn't need a thing done to it. But tell the fool he must pull himself together and take care not to let my property be damaged by the first little brute who comes along. Tell 'im to find their fathers and have 'em talk to you if he doesn't do so himself."

On the way back a frightened rabbit crossed the track, Don Batassano's horse shied, kicked out, and the magnate, who had a fine little English saddle but insisted on twisted ropes instead of stirrups, ended on the ground. He was not hurt and Giacomino, well used to this situation, took the mare by the bridle and held it firm; from the ground Don Batassano whipped mercilessly up at the nose, eyes, flanks of the animal, which was taken by a continuous quiver and beginning to foam. A kick in its belly ended the pedagogic operation, Don Batassano remounted, and the pair returned home just as it was growing dark.

Meanwhile Ferrara, unaware that the master of the house was out, had gone into the study and, finding it empty, sat down a moment to wait. The room contained a gun-rack with two rifles, a shelf with a few boxes ("Taxes", "Title deeds", "Cautions", "Mortgages", said the labels stuck on brown cardboard); on the desk was the deed-of-sale signed two hours before; behind, on the wall, that map.

The accountant got up to look closer: from his professional knowledge, from the innumerable indiscretions to which he had listened, he well knew how that vast property had been put together: it had been an epopee of cunning and perfidy, of ruthlessness and defiance of law, of luck too and of daring. Ferrara thought how interesting it would be to see a map in different colours showing successive acquisitions, as school text-books do the expansion of the House of Savoy. Here at Gibilmonte was the embryo: six measures of corn, half a hectare of vines and a three-roomed hut, all that had been inherited by Don Batassano's father, Gaspare, analphabetic of genius. In early youth he had seduced the deaf-and-dumb daughter of a smallholder scarcely less poor than himself, and doubled his holding with the dowry obtained by compulsory marriage. His wife, handicapped as she was, entered into her husband's game completely: by grinding thrift the couple accumulated a hoard which though tiny was precious in a place like Sicily, where hoarding at that period, as in the city-states of antiquity, was based exclusively on usury.

Shrewd loans had been granted, loans of a particular kind which are made to people with property but insufficient income to pay interest. The lowing of Marta, Gaspare's wife, going round the village at dusk to exact her weekly dues became proverbial. "When Marta's agrunting, homes go atumbling." In ten years of gesticulating visits, in ten years of extorting crops from the Marchese Santapau whose mezzadro, or share-cropper, Gaspare was, in ten years of cautiously moved boundaries, in ten years of contented starvation, the couple's property had multiplied fivefold: he was only twenty-eight, the present Don Batassano seven. There had been a rough patch when the Bourbon legal authorities took it into their heads to inquire about one of the many corpses found out in the country: Gaspare had to keep away from Gibilmonte, and his wife gave out that he was staying with a cousin at Adernò to learn about mulberry growing; in reality every single night from a nearby hill the doting Gaspare had watched smoke rising from the kitchen of his happy little home. Then came the Thousand, everything was upside down, inconvenient papers vanished from legal offices, and Gaspare Ibba returned home officially.

Everything was better than before. It was then that Gaspare thought up a move which seemed mad, like every stroke of genius; just as Napoleon at Austerlitz dared to divest his centre in order to trap the Austro-Russian boobies between very strong flanks, so Gaspare mortgaged all his hard-fought land up to the hilt, and with the few thousand lire raised by this operation made a loan without interest to the Marchese Santapau, who was in difficulties due to donations to the Bourbon cause. The result was: two years later the Santapau lost their estate of Balate,[1] which they had anyway never seen and from its name took to be sterile, all mortgages were off the Ibba property, Gaspare had become "Don Gaspare" and goatsmeat was eaten at his home on Saturdays and Sundays. On reaching the goal of the first hundred thousand lire all went with the precision of a mechanical instrument; ecclesiastical properties were acquired for a tenth of their value by paying the first two instalments of their wretched assessment; their buildings, the springs nearby, the rights-of-way enclosed, made it much easier to buy up surrounding lay properties that had lost value; the large incomes accruing went to the purchase or expropriation of other more distant land.

So when Don Gaspare died still young his property was already of notable size; but, like the Prussian territories in the middle of the eighteenth century, it consisted of large islands separated by the properties of others. To the son Batassano, as to Frederick the Second, fell the task and the glory, first of unifying all in one single block then of moving the boundaries of the block itself towards more distant areas. Vineyards, olive and almond-groves, pastures, ground-rents, sowing-land particularly, were annexed and digested, the income flowing into the shabby office at Gibilmonte where they stayed for a very short time and whence they soon issued, almost intact, to be transformed back into more land. A wind of uninterrupted good fortune swelled the sails of the Ibba galleon: the name began to be pronounced with reverence throughout the whole poverty-stricken triangle of the

[1] Sicilian-Calabrian word, from Arabic, meaning "paving-slab". (Trs.)

island. Don Batassano meanwhile had married at the age of thirty, and not a handicapped creature like his venerated mother but a buxom girl of eighteen called Laura, daughter of the Gibilmonte notary; as dowry she brought her own health, a considerable sum in ready cash, her father's valuable experience with the Curia, and an utter submission once her own considerable sexual needs were satisfied. Living proof of this submission of hers was eight children; rough sunless happiness reigned in the Ibba household.

The accountant Ferrara was a person of sensitive feelings, a human species very rare in Sicily. His father had been an employee of the Salina administration in the stormy days of old Prince Fabrizio; and he himself, raised in the padded atmosphere of that household, had been accustomed to desiring a life commonplace indeed, but calm; his own little sliver of princely cheese to nibble was enough for him. Those two big square metres of oiled paper evoked harsh and stubborn struggles within his soul, more a rodent's than a carnivore's. An impression came to him that he was re-reading instalments of La Cecilia's *History of the Bourbons of Naples* which his father, an advanced liberal, used to buy him every Saturday. Here at Gibilmonte, of course, were none of the imaginary orgies of Caserta described in that tract: here all was ruggedly, positively, puritanically evil. He took fright and left the room.

That evening at supper the whole family was present except for the eldest son Gaspare, who was in Palermo with the excuse of preparing to retake his school-leaving exams (he was already twenty). The meal was served with rustic simplicity; all the cutlery, heavy and rich, was heaped in the middle of the table and everyone fished about in the pile according to need; the manservant Totò and the maidservant Mariannina insisted on serving from the right. Signora Laura was a picture of health in supreme flowering, that is in major rotundity; her well-shaped chin, her pretty nose, her eyes expert in connubial delights, vanished into an exuberance of still fresh, firm and appetising fat; the enormous bulk of her body was covered in black silk, emblem of mourning perpetually renewed. Her sons Melchiorre, Pietro and Ignazio, her daughters Marta, Franceschina, Assunta and Paolina, showed alternating similarities, peculiar combinations of the rapacious features of their father and the clement ones of their mother. None, male or female, had any taste whatsoever in dress: the girls were in printed cretonnes (grey on white), the boys in sailor suits, even the eldest among those present, Melchiorre, whose budding seventeen-year-old moustache gave him an odd air of some member of a Royal suite. The conversation, or rather the dialogue, between Don Batassano and Ferrara ranged exclusively around two subjects: the price of land in the neighbourhood of Palermo compared to that in the neighbourhood of Gibilmonte, and gossip about aristocratic Palermo society. Don Batassano considered all those nobles as "starving", even those who after all, if only in collections of antiques apart from incomes, had fortunes equal to his own. Always shut away in his own parts, with rare trips to the local town and very rare journeys to Palermo in order to "follow" law-cases in the Courts, he did not know even one of these nobles personally, and had created an abstract and monotonic image of them, like that of the public for Harlequin or Captain Fracassa. Prince A. was a spendthrift, Prince B. a womaniser, Duke C. violent, Baron D. a gambler, Don Giuseppe E. a bully, Marchese F. "aesthetic" (he meant an "aesthete", a euphemism in its turn for something worse) and so on; each was a contemptible figure cut in cardboard. These opinions of Don Batassano's had a formidable propensity to error, and it might be said that there was no epithet which was not coupled erroneously to a name, and certainly no defect which was not fabulously exaggerated, while the real defects of these persons remained unknown to him: obviously his mind worked in abstractions and took pleasure in contrasting the purity of the Ibbas with the corrupt background of the old nobility.

Ferrara knew rather more about these things, though with lacunae too, so that when he tried to contradict the more fantastic assertions he ran out of arguments; also his words aroused such moralistic indignation in Don Batassano that he soon fell silent. But anyway they had now reached the end of the meal.

This, Ferrara considered, had been excellent; Donna Laura did not abandon herself to Pindaric flights in matters of food: she had Sicilian dishes served, as numerous and highly flavoured as possible and so murderous. Macaroni literally swam in oil of their own sauce and were buried under avalanches of *cacciocavallo* cheese, meat was stuffed with incendiary salami, trifle or "*zuppa in fretta*" contained triple the cochineal, sugar and candied fruit prescribed. But to Ferrara all that, as has been said, seemed exquisite and the apex of a really good table; at his rare luncheons in the Salina household he had always been disappointed by the insipidity of the food. Next day, though, on return to Palermo, after handing over to Prince Fabrizietto the 78,400 lire, he described the meal offered him and as he knew the prince's predilection for "*coulis de volaille*" at the Pré-Catalan and "*timbales d'écrevisses*" at Prunier's, he made sound horrible what he had in fact thought excellent. Thus he gave much pleasure to Salina who, during his "little game of poker" at the club later on, described every detail to his friends, ever avid for news of the legendary Ibbas; and all laughed till a moment when Peppino San Carlo announced impassively that he had a full-house of queens.

As has been said, there was acute curiosity about the Ibba family in the noble circles of Palermo. Curiosity is, after all, the mother of fables, and from it during those years were born hundreds of fantasies about that sudden fortune. These bore witness not only to the frothy and infantile imaginations of the upper classes, but also to an unconscious unease at seeing that a great fortune could be built up exclusively in land at the beginning of the twentieth century, this being a form of wealth which, in the bitter experience of each of those gentlemen, was demolition material unsuited to the construction of rich buildings. Those same landed proprietors felt that this modern reincarnation, in the Ibbas, of the vast grain-bearing estates of the Chiaramonte and the Ventimiglia families of past centuries was irrational and dangerous for themselves, so they were all secretly against it; and that not only because this imposing edifice was erected largely from material which had once belonged to themselves, but because they took it as a sign of the permanent anachronism which is the brake on the wheels of the Sicilian cart, an anachronism realised by many but which no one, in fact, can evade or avoid collaborating with.

It should be repeated that this unease remained latent in their collective unconscious: it flowered only in the guise of jests and funny stories, as might be expected of a class with a low consumption of general ideas. A first and most elementary form of these was an exaggeration in figures, which with us are always elastic. Batassano Ibba's fortune, though easy to check, was valued at dozens of million lire; one bold spirit even dared once to speak of "nearly a billion", but the effect was as if he had remained silent, for this sum, to-day so banal, was in such rare use in 1901 that nearly everyone was ignorant of its true meaning, and in those days of gold lire the phrase "a billion lire" meant really nothing at all. Analogous fantasies were woven about the origins of this fortune: the humbleness of Don Batassano's origins were difficult to exaggerate, (old Corrado Finale, whose mother was a Santapau, had hinted without saying so openly that Don Batassano was the son of a brother-in-law of his who had been in residence for some time at Gibilmonte; but the story found little credit because Finale was known to have a habit of attributing to himself or to his relatives the clandestine parentage of any celebrity mentioned, whether victorious general or acclaimed prima donna); that modest corpse, though, which had been such a bother to Don Gaspare, was multiplied tenfold, a hundredfold, and every "elimination" that had taken place in Sicily over the last thirty years (and there had been quite a number) was put down to the Ibbas, who were, after all, legally unimpeachable. This, surprising though it may seem, was the legend's most benevolent part because deeds of violence when unpunished were at that time a motive for esteem, the halo of Sicilian saints being blood-red.

To these fantasies grown from seed were added others grafted;

for instance out came, refurbished, a tale told a hundred years before about Testasecca, who caused a little channel to be scooped, collected his hundreds of cows and thousands of sheep on a hillock above, and had them milked all at the same moment, so presenting King Ferdinand IV with the sight of a small stream of milk flowing warm and frothing at his feet. This fable, which is not without a certain pastoral poetry that should have suggested its origin to be in Theocritus, was now adapted to Don Batassano by the simple substitution of King Umberto I of Italy for King Ferdinand of the Two Sicilies; and though it was quite easy to prove that the former sovereign had never set foot on any Ibba land this persisted, unrefuted.

It was for these reasons of rancour mingled with fear that, when the "little game of poker" was over, conversation again fell on the subject of the Ibbas. The dozen members present had settled down on the terrace of the club, which overlooked a placid courtyard and was shaded by a tall tree raining petals of lilac down on those gentlemen, most of whom were old. Footmen in red and blue brought round ices and cool soft drinks. From the depths of a wicker armchair came the ever choleric tones of Santa Giulia. "Well, could someone please tell me how much land these blessed Ibbas really do own?"

"Someone could, and will. Fourteen thousand three hundred and twenty-five hectares," replied San Carlo coldly.

"Is that all? I thought more."

"Fourteen thousand, balls! People who have been there say they can't be less than twenty thousand hectares, sure as death and taxes; and all first class crop-bearing land."

General Làscari, who seemed immersed in reading *La Tribuna*, brusquely lowered the newspaper and showed his liverish visage embroidered with yellow lines in which very white eyeballs showed up hard and rather sinister, like the eyes of some Greek bronzes. "Twenty-eight thousand hectares they are, neither less nor more; I was told by my nephew who is a cousin of the local Prefect's wife. That's it, once and for all; there's no need to discuss the matter any longer."

Pippo Follonica, a visiting guest from Rome, burst out laughing. "But if you're all so interested why not send someone down to the Land Registry? It's easy to know the truth, this truth anyway."

This rational suggestion received a cold reception. Follonica did not understand the passionate, non-statistical nature of the discussion; these gentlemen were tossing about among themselves envies, rancours and anxieties, all emotions which no Land Registry certificates could assuage.

The general grew furious. "When I tell you something there's no need for any registry whatsoever." Then politeness towards a guest softened him. "My dear prince, you don't know what our Land Registry office is like! Transfers of property are never recorded and people still figure as owners who've sold up long ago and are now in the Poor House."

Faced with so detailed a denial, Follonica changed tactics. "Let's admit that the number of hectares remains unknown; what must be known is the value of property in the hands of this boor who excites you all so much!"

"Perfectly well known; eight million exactly."

"Balls!" That was the inevitable opening to any phrase from Santa Giulia, "Balls! Not a cent less than twelve!"

"What a world you live in! You don't know anything! There's twenty-five million in land alone. Then there are ground-rents, capital on loan and not yet transformed into property, the value of cattle. Another five million at least." The general had put down his newspaper and was getting worked up. His peremptory manner had for years irritated the entire club, each member of which wished to be the only one making incontrovertible affirmations; so that a coalition of reawakened antipathies at once formed against his opinion, and without any reference to major or minor truths the estimate of the Ibba property slumped. "That's all poetic nonsense; about money and sanctity, believe half a half, as the proverb goes. If Batassano Ibba has ten million all told that's more than enough." The figure had been distilled from nothing at all, that is from polemical necessity; but when spoken, as it responded to everyone's wishes, it calmed down all except the general, who went on gesticulating from deep in his armchair, impotent against his nine adversaries.

A footman entered carrying a long wooden pole at the end of which was a wick dipped in spirit. The gentle light of dusk changed to the harsh glare of a gas chandelier.

The guest from Rome was much amused: it was his first visit to Sicily, and during the five days of his stay in Palermo he had been invited to a number of houses and had begun to change his opinions about what he had presumed to be the provincialism of Palermo; dinners had been well-served, drawing-rooms splendid, ladies graceful. But now this impassioned discussion about the fortune of an individual whom none of the contestants knew or wanted to know, these patent exaggerations, this convulsive gesticulating about nothing, made him reverse, reminded him a little too closely of conversations heard at Fondi or Palestrina when he had to go out there to see about his estates, or maybe even at the chemist Bésuquet's of which he had preserved a happy memory since his reading of *Tartarin*:[1] and he began laying in a store of tales to regale friends on his return to Rome a week later. But he was wrong; too much a man of fashion ever to probe much deeper than the obvious, what appeared to him as a humorous exhibition of provincialism was anything but comic: this was the tragic jerking of a class which was watching the end of its own land-owning supremacy, that is of its own reason for existence and its own social continuity, and in these wilful exaggerations and artificial diminutions sought outlets for its anger, relief for its fear.

The truth being impossible to establish, the conversation deviated: it was still investigating Batassano Ibba's private affairs but now turned to consider his personal life.

"He lives like a monk; gets up at four in the morning; goes out into the market-place to engage day-labourers, is busy with

---

[1] *Tartarin de Tarascon* by Alphonse Daudet.

estate-management the whole day long, eats nothing but pasta and vegetables in oil, and is in bed by eight."

Salina protested, "A monk with a wife and eight children, let's remember. One of my employees spent forty-eight hours at his house: it's ugly but it's big and comfortable, decent enough; the wife seems to have been pretty, the children well-dressed; in fact one of them is here in Palermo to study and the food at his table is heavy but plentiful, as I've already told you."

The general stuck to his guns: "You, Salina, believe everything you're told, or rather, they wanted to throw dust in the eyes of your man, who must be an idiot. Bread, cheese and oil-lamps, that's Ibba's daily routine, his real life; when someone comes from Palermo he obviously tries to put up a show, to dazzle us so he deludes himself."

Santa Giulia, under the impetus of the news he wanted to communicate, was jumping about in his armchair; his well-shod feet banged the floor, his hands trembled, and the ash of his cigarette snowed all over his suit. "Balls, Gentlemen! Gentlemen, balls! You're utterly mistaken. I'm the only one who really knows about this: the wife of one of my keepers comes from Torrebella a few steps from Gibilmonte; every now and again she goes to see her sister who is married there and has told her everything. One can't be more certain than that, I think." He sought for a confirmation of his own certainty in everyone's eyes and, as all were amused, easily found it. Although there was no bashful ear to be respected he lowered his voice: without this melodramatic preamble the effect of his revelations would never be the same.

"Three miles from Gibilmonte, Don Batassano has had a small house built; the most luxurious little place imaginable, furnished by Salci and all that." Reminiscences of reading Catulle Mendès, nostalgic memories of Parisian brothels, yearnings, unrealised though long nursed, stirred his imagination. "He had Rochegrosse come from Paris to fresco all the rooms: the great painter was three months at Gibilmonte and demanded a hundred thousand lire a month." (Rochegrosse had in fact been in Sicily two years before: he had remained a week with his wife and three children, and left again after quietly visiting the Capella Palatina, Segesta, and the Latomie of Syracuse.) "It cost a fortune! But what frescoes he did! Enough to bring a dead man to life! Naked women, quite naked, dancing, drinking and coupling with men and with each other in every position, in every conceivable manner. Masterpieces! An encyclopedia, I tell you, an encyclopedia of pleasures! Just let a Parisian loose with a hundred thousand lire a month! There Ibba receives women by the dozen; Italians, French, German, Spanish. La Otero was there too, I know that for a fact. That fellow Batassano has made his *Parc aux Cerfs* there, like Louis the Fifteenth."

This time Santa Giulia really had caused a sensation: everyone sat listening to him open-mouthed. Not that he was believed, but they found this fantasy a highly poetic one, and each longed to have Ibba's millions so that others could invent similar splendid nonsense about himself. The first to shake off the spell was the general: "And how d'you come to know that? Have you been into the house yourself, pray? As odalisque or eunuch?" They laughed, Santa Giulia laughed too. "I told you; the wife of my keeper Antonio has seen those paintings."

"Fine! Then you've a keeper who's a cuckold."

"Cuckold, balls! She went there to take some sheets which she'd washed. They didn't let her in but a window was open and she saw it all."

The castle of lies was obviously of extreme fragility; but it was of such beauty, with its female thighs and nameless obscenities, its famous painters and hundred-thousand-lire notes, that no one had any desire to give it a puff and bring it down.

Salina pulled out his watch, "Mamma Mia! Eight o'clock already! I must go home and dress; there's *Traviata* to-night at the Politeama, and Bellincioni's *Amami Alfredo* is not to be missed. See you in the club-box!"

JOY AND THE LAW

[DECEMBER 1956–JANUARY 1957]

When he boarded the bus he got in everyone's way.

There was his briefcase crammed with other people's papers, the enormous parcel bulging out under his left arm, his plush grey scarf, his umbrella on the point of flying open: everything conspired to obstruct his showing his return ticket. He was obliged to rest the great package on the conductor's ledge, provoking an avalanche of small change; he tried bending down to pick up all this insubstantial coinage, rousing those behind him to cries of protest – they were desperate in case his dilly-dallying left them with their coat-tails caught in the automatic doors. He managed to insert himself into the line of strap-hangers; he was slight of build, but what with his paraphernalia he had all the corpulence of a nun bundled up in seven habits. As the bus skated through the slush amid the dreary welter of traffic, the sheer awkwardness of his bulk sent a wave of disgruntlement from one end of the vehicle to the other: he trod on toes and got his own trodden on, he occasioned remonstrations, and when he even overheard, behind his back, three syllables alluding to his presumed conjugal infelicities, honour required him to turn his head, and he liked to imagine that his lacklustre eyes were charged with menace.

Meanwhile they were travelling through streets of rustic baroque frontages that concealed a hinterland whose squalor was at all events exposed at every corner. The ochre lights of eighty-year-old shops slid by.

On reaching his stop he rang the bell, alighted, tripped over his umbrella and finally found himself in sole possession of his square metre of dislocated pavement; he hastened to check that he had his plastic wallet. And he was free to relish his own happiness.

Contained inside the wallet were thirty-seven thousand two hundred and forty-five lire, his Christmas bonus (comprising an extra month's pay) remitted to him an hour ago – in other words the removal of several thorns: that of the landlord, all the more insistent because his was a controlled rent and he had two quarters' owing; that of the most punctual collector of the instalments on his wife's "chinchilla" jacket ("It suits you far better than a full-length coat, darling; it makes you look more svelte"); that of the black looks from the fishmonger and the greengrocer. Those four high-denomination notes also disposed of the worries over the next light bill, the anxious glances at the children's shoes, the nervous scrutiny of the fluttering flames on the bottled gas. The notes did not represent opulence – far from it! – but they promised a respite from worry, and that is the true joy of the poor. A couple of thousand would, moreover, survive for a moment to be expended in the splendour of the Christmas dinner.

But he had received plenty of Christmas bonuses in his time, and the rose-tinted euphoria that now buoyed him up was not to be attributed to the fleeting exhilaration that *they* elicited. Pink of hue, indeed, like the wrapping on the gentle burden that was bringing an ache to his left arm. It stemmed, in fact, from the seven-kilo *panettone* he had brought home from the office. Not that he was mad about that mixture (however highly guaranteed, nay, however dubious) of flour, sugar, powdered egg and raisins. On the contrary, deep down, he did not care for it. But seven kilos'-worth of luxury all at one go! an abundance at once circumscribed and boundless for a household whose sustenance generally arrived by the hundred grammes and half litres! A high-class product in a larder dedicated to the labels of third-rate goods! What a pleasure for Maria! What a lark for the children, who would spend a fortnight on the trails of that unexplored El Dorado, an afternoon snack!

These, however, were the joys of others, material joys

comprised of vanilla essence and coloured cardboard, in other words, *panettone*. His private happiness was quite different, it was a spiritual joy, compounded of pride and tenderness; yessirs, a spiritual joy.

When, a little earlier, the Managing Director had handed out the pay envelopes and Christmas greetings with the supercilious bonhomie of the old party boss that he was, he had added that the seven-kilo *panettone*, sent in to the office as a gift from the Big-Time Production Company, would be allotted to the most deserving employee, and so he asked his dear colleagues if they would democratically (that was his word) designate the fortunate man there and then.

Meanwhile there sat the *panettone*, in the middle of the desk, inert, hermetically sealed, ("cumbered with portent" as the same official would have put it twenty years earlier) in its cloth lining. The colleagues muttered and sniggered; then they all of them, led by the Managing Director, had shouted his name. A great satisfaction, an assurance of the continuation of his employment, in a word, a triumph. And nothing had succeeded in shaking that tonic sensation, neither the three hundred lire he had been obliged to fork out in the bar downstairs, in the doubly livid light of the stormy sunset and the low-wattage neon, when he had stood his friends coffee, nor the weight of the booty, nor the scurrilous words overheard on the bus; nothing, not even when there flashed in the depths of his mind the notion that his fellows had all been engaged in an act of disdainful pity for his indigence. He was, in truth, too poor to permit the weed of vanity to sprout where it had no business.

He made his way home along a street to whose decrepitude the air-raids, fifteen years earlier, had put the finishing touches. He reached the spectral piazza at the end of which crouched his ghostly dwelling.

But he gave the hall-porter Cosimo a cheery greeting, though the man despised him in the knowledge that the bookkeeper earned even less than he did. Nine steps, three steps, nine steps up to Mr Bigshot's floor. Pooh! What if he did drive a *millecento* – his wife was an old trollop and ugly too. Nine steps, three steps, whoops!, nine steps up to Dr Thingummy's residence. Worse yet! A bone idle son who was crazy about motorcycles; besides, his waiting-room was always empty. Nine steps, three steps, nine steps: his own apartment. Here lived a man who was well liked, honest, highly regarded, his merits rewarded, a peerless accountant.

He opened the door, stepped into the tiny entrance hall permeated with the odour of sautéed onion; on a chest no bigger than a hamper he deposited the dead weight of the parcel, the briefcase pregnant with other people's concerns, the cumbersome muffler. His voice piped up: "Maria! Come quickly! Come and see what I've got!"

His wife came out of the kitchen in a housecoat soiled from the pots and pans; her little hands, reddened from rinsing the dishes, rested on her belly deformed from child-bearing. The runny-nosed infants crowded, chirruping, about the pink phenomenon but dared not touch it.

"Well done! And your pay, have you brought it? I don't have so much as a lira left."

"Here it is, darling; I'm keeping back only the small change, two hundred and forty-five lire. But take a look at this abundance!"

Maria used to be adorable and until a few years ago she had the liveliest little face, lit up by a mischievous pair of eyes. Now the rows with shopkeepers had coarsened her voice, the unwhole-some fare had ruined her complexion, the incessant scrutiny of a future of looming fog and reefs had dowsed the sparkle in her eyes. All that survived in her was a saintly spirit and therefore inflexible and devoid of tenderness, a deep goodness constrained to find expression in rebukes and prohibitions. There was also a tenacious if chastened pride of caste, because her uncle was a leading hatter in Via Indipendenza and she disdained the origins (quite, quite other) of her Girolamo whom she still adored as one dotes on a stupid but lovable child.

Her glance slid indifferently over the decorative box. "That's good. Tomorrow we'll send it to Avvocato Risma. We owe him a favour."

A couple of years ago the lawyer had entrusted him with a complex job of bookkeeping and, in addition to paying him for it, he had invited them both to dinner in his apartment, all abstract art and tubular-steel furniture, during which the accountant had been in agony with the new shoes he had bought especially. And now, thanks to this lawyer who did not lack for anything, his Maria, his Andrea, his Saverio, their little Giuseppina, he himself, had to sacrifice the one and only vein of abundance they had struck in all those years!

He dashed into the kitchen, seized a knife and lunged to cut the gilded string gracefully tied round the package by some industrious Milanese factory-girl. But a raw red hand tapped him wearily on the shoulder: "Girolamo, don't be a baby. You know we have to return Risma's favour."

It was The Law speaking, The Law handed down by irreproachable hatters.

"But darling, this is a reward, it is evidence of merit, an acknowledgement of standing!"

"Never mind. They're a fine lot, those colleagues of yours and their delicate feelings! It's charity, Girò, nothing more than charity." She called him by her old affectionate nickname, and smiled at him with eyes in which none but he could detect the erstwhile charms.

"Tomorrow you can buy another *panettone*, a little one, that'll do for us; and four of those pink corkscrew candles on display at Standa;[1] that'll make it quite festive."

So the next day he bought an anonymous *panettone*, not four but two of those amazing candles and, through an agency, sent the Phenomenon to Avvocato Risma, which cost him a further two hundred lire.

After Christmas, furthermore, he was obliged to buy a third *panettone*, and bring it, sliced up for disguise, to his colleagues who

---

[1] A chainstore for thrifty shoppers, similar to Woolworth. (Trs.)

had been teasing him for not giving them so much as a crumb of the original prize.

As for the original *panettone*, a pall of mist descended upon it.

He went to the "Lightning" agency to complain. The despatch note was offhandedly shown to him – the lawyer's domestic's signature on it was upside down. After Twelfth Night, however, a visiting card arrived "with heartiest thanks and good wishes".

Honour was satisfied.

Introduction to the Literary Sections

DAVID GILMOUR

The Prince of Lampedusa never pursued a working career. In 1913 he enrolled reluctantly as a law student with a view to becoming a diplomat like his uncle Pietro. But military service in the First World War interrupted his studies and, on demobilisation in 1920, he declined to resume them. Subsequently he had no conventional employment until 1944 when he was appointed President of the Red Cross in the province of Palermo. After his resignation two years later, he lapsed once more into lethargy before deciding to dedicate the last thirty months of his life to writing.

Yet Lampedusa's long periods of indolence were not spent frivolously in upper-class Sicilian society. Shy, awkward and short of money, he had no interest in night-clubs, casinos or motor-cars. Until his marriage at the age of thirty-five – and at intervals afterwards – he lived quietly with his parents in Palermo and devoted most of his time to reading. As his friend Francesco Orlando recalled after his death, "literature was the great occupation and consolation of this nobleman from whom various patrimonial misfortunes had removed all worldliness and practical usefulness, and who was reduced to living isolated, without any luxury other than his considerable expenditure on books. . ."

Lampedusa never moved anywhere without a book. According to his widow, he always carried a copy of Shakespeare so that he could "console himself when he saw something disagreeable"; at his bedside he kept *The Pickwick Papers* to comfort him during sleepless nights. Friends used to encounter him in Palermitan cafés eating cakes and reading a volume of French Renaissance poetry, or wandering around the city with a bag stuffed with courgettes and volumes of Proust. Once he read an entire novel by Balzac without moving from his favourite café, the Pasticceria del Massimo. In the evenings he and his wife often read aloud – in the original language – passages from their favourite European authors.

Lampedusa's love of books was stimulated by a solitary childhood and by personal timidity. Although prevented by an unsympathetic father from reading literature at university, he continued his studies informally at home. Before visiting England in his twenties he had read Shakespeare's entire works and must have been one of the first Italians to penetrate Joyce. His interest in literature was so consuming that he devoured minor writers as comprehensively as their superiors. Literature was like a forest, he once said, in which it was important to investigate not just the large trees but the undergrowth and wild flowers as well. They were all part of the great body of literature and contributed to each other's growth. He regarded Horace Walpole's *The Castle of Otranto* as "not worth a cigarette butt" in itself but considered it an important book because it opened the way to novels by Scott and Thackeray, to the supernatural writing of Poe and to certain works of Henry James.

In his mid-fifties Lampedusa regretted that he had read almost everything and envied younger friends who had so much literature yet to enjoy. But he went to great lengths to discover new authors for himself, even to the extent of learning Spanish so that he could read Calderón and Góngora. And he basked in his esoteric knowledge of remote corners of literature. After talking to various writers at a literary congress in 1954, he noted privately that he was "mathematically certain of being the only person in Italy to have read" the obscure English writer Martin Tupper.

French was Lampedusa's first foreign language and the idiom in which he corresponded with his wife. Although he enjoyed making jokes about French greed and dirtiness, he loved France and her literature. Montaigne, he believed, was her finest prose writer and Stendhal her greatest literary figure. While Dickens was probably Lampedusa's favourite novelist, Stendhal was the one he admired most, and his analysis of the Frenchman's craft has been included in this volume.

The Sicilian's Francophilia was exceeded, however, by his love for England, a country with which he recognised closer ties of temperament. He began to visit London in the 1920s when his uncle – the only member of his family to have a career – was the Italian ambassador. Lampedusa did not care for diplomatic society but he explored with enthusiasm the landscapes he already knew through literature. He loved watching Shakespeare's plays in the West End, browsing through second-hand bookstalls in the Charing Cross Road, and relaxing in the leather armchairs of a private library, a tea-table at his side and a bulky volume in his hand. He also made excursions into the countryside, usually to destinations with literary or historical associations; a Sicilian friend later teased him for having visited "every" house in England where a writer had lived.

Lampedusa once claimed he was "not blind to the many defects of the English character", but the only ones he listed were "smugness" and intolerance of the unconventional behaviour of the country's Romantic poets. On another occasion he told his wife he had an English temperamant, and he did indeed have some of the qualities he believed the English possessed: their reserve, their self-control, their ironic sense of humour. He was impressed by certain concepts and phrases such as "fair play" and "the underdog", which led him to make favourable comparisons with the Sicilians. Other unSicilian characteristics he admired were understatement and a self-deprecating sense of humour.

Lampedusa did not visit England during the last twenty years of his life, but he kept in touch with her literary developments despite the frustrations involved in trying to procure the latest works of Graham Greene or T. S. Eliot in Palermo. At the end of 1953, about a year before he began writing *The Leopard*, his wife suggested he gave an informal course on English literature to two young Sicilian friends, Francesco Orlando and Gioacchino Lanza. Lampedusa was delighted by the idea which gave him, as the Princess later explained, "a pretext for re-reading authors almost unknown to Italian teaching and allowed young people to share those interests which had given him so many pleasurable hours".

He prepared the lessons with care, writing them out in full before his pupils arrived on three evenings a week. Occasionally attended by other young friends, they continued for a year, filling a thousand pages of manuscript covering the entire range of English literature between Chaucer and Greene. From time to time he doubted whether the exercise was worthwhile and expressed dissatisfaction with what he had said. Some sections, he declared, were "the worst pages that had ever been written by a human pen" and those on Byron's life were an "endless abomination". To his pupils he pretended that he was burning the manuscript after each lesson, but fortunately it survives, the most important existing document on his life.

The full text was published in two volumes by Mondadori in 1990 and 1991. Lampedusa would have been horrified – as indeed would any writer – to learn that his subjective and whimsical views, jotted down without reference books on warm Sicilian afternoons, would be scrupulously edited (by Lanza's second wife Nicoletta) and issued by a leading Italian publisher – the very one which in his lifetime had rejected *The Leopard*. Yet the book cannot damage his reputation so long as it is read not as a polished work of literary criticism but as an essay on a country he loved and as a very personal document that reveals much about its author, his tastes, his character and his sense of humour.

The book is full of idiosyncrasies which are often bizarre, usually illuminating and always delightful. Lampedusa used his lessons to exhort his young friends not only to read books but also to set their horizons beyond the provincial world of Sicily. Conrad, he told them, should be read "as an antidote to the unbearable stagnation of Palermitan life". He also tried to explain "nonsense" verse to his listeners, though without illusions of their capacity to see its point: "clouds of smoke from the stakes of the

Counter-Reformation", he feared, still hung too heavily over Palermo for them to be able to appreciate Edward Lear and Lewis Carroll.

By the time he had completed the lessons, Lampedusa was labouring at the first chapter of *The Leopard*. But his new pedagogic enthusiasm impelled him to begin immediately a course in French literature. It was shorter and less comprehensive than its predecessor and did not attempt to reveal the entire panorama of a nation's literature since the formation of its language. Concentrating on certain periods, he dealt in detail with the sixteenth century and part of the seventeenth but omitted the eighteenth altogether because he feared he would be bored writing about it. From the nineteenth century he gave lessons on only a few writers, devoting to Stendhal almost as much time as he had given to Shakespeare the year before. Like André Gide, he hesitated a long time before deciding which of Stendhal's masterpieces was the greatest novel in any language. Finally he chose *La Chartreuse de Parme*: "Written by an old man for old people, one has to be over forty before one can understand it. Then one sees that this book, bare even of artistic illusions, almost bare of adjectives, nostalgic, ironic, self-possessed and gentle, is the summit of all world fiction."

The extracts published in this volume are only fragments of Lampedusa's lessons, not much more than five per cent of the total. Yet the French and the English sections are broadly representative of the author's different approaches to the literature of the two countries. In the tutorials on Stendhal he committed himself to a rigorous examination of the writer's style, analysing the technique that produced the great novels. But with England, which he regarded as "the country least governed by logic", he made less effort at analysis, abandoning himself to an indulgent spree among authors he loved and whom he wished to introduce to his pupils. A shy man unable to communicate easily with people when he was in England, he found consolation in close acquaintanceship with fictional characters. For Lampedusa, Falstaff and Micawber were as real as Shakespeare and Dickens, quintessential Englishmen and vicarious friends. He would have sacrificed ten years of his life, he once said with feeling, for the privilege of meeting Sir John Falstaff.

ENGLISH LITERATURE

Author's Introduction

Some words of introduction, beginning with a word of apology. My boldness in giving tutorials in English literature can only be pardoned if you take into account my devotion to that literature. Secondly, a word of explanation. This is not a written work, or it is only in the sense that it is a shorthand record. My memory is so uncertain that without these notes I would remember half the things I wanted to say only when my listeners were already on their way out. It is thus a shorthand record in advance, nothing more than jottings of words.

I have two or three histories of English literature within reach, but I have scrupulously avoided looking at them. What you will hear is only the sum of my memories and my impressions. Hence the errors and inaccuracies, perhaps blunders, which you will notice without difficulty; hence also the digressions and "tangents" which abound; yet if I had merely conversed, they would have been even more numerous.

These notes are only the residue, the precipitate of thirty years of disordered reading passed through a brain notorious for its forgetfulness. Consequently you have little to hope for.

Half the pages of the first part are dedicated to Shakespeare. He is the author I know least superficially, and I want to discuss the sonnets[1] almost individually and all the plays without exception. Yet these are not notes on Shakespeare but notes about my Shakespearian memories, a very different matter. A bucket of seawater is not the sea. To know the sea, one needs to sound it, navigate it and even run the risk of shipwreck. That will be your task...

---

[1] Lampedusa dealt at length with the sonnets, concluding that, while about half of them had little artistic value, thirty of the others had beautiful lines, and the "remaining forty were among the finest things in world literature".

I

Shakespeare

The Betrayals of Falstaff

Henry IV in its two parts is the masterpiece of Shakespeare's historical dramas. Great as a whole and great in parts, it contains neither a mediocre scene nor a misdrawn character. Regarding the whole, there is something both moving and magnificent in the contrast between the scenes of humble tavern life, so full of vitality, and those melancholic moments at which the King appears, that suspicious, betrayed monarch whom we have already met in *Richard II*, that bold, "pushing" King of cutting words known as Bolingbroke. And amid these painful scenes are the parentheses formed by the appearances of Hotspur, the enthusiastic rebel, full of brio and good humour, who is forever giving his anxious wife a farewell kiss.

But the gem of all the characters, needless to say, is Falstaff, gem of goodness knows how many carats, one of the three or four greatest Shakespearian characters. Adorable rogue, man of fine and unconquerable spirit, peerless creation of the highest wit – anyone of us would give ten years for the privilege of spending an hour with him. "I am not only witty in myself but the cause that wit is in other men." This is probably the key to Shakespeare's outstanding success (of which the echoes have reached us) as a conversationist in the Mermaid Tavern. And a benign Providence has enabled a considerable even if insufficient portion of this tavern talk to reach us through Falstaff himself. From the instant he appears on the scene accompanied by that extraordinary image of the sun ("A fair hot wench in flame-coloured taffeta") until the moment he waits for the new King's procession, his appearance heralds the most serene happiness that one can enjoy. Through the scenes of highway robbery ("Go, hang thyself in thine own heir-apparent garters"), the exaggerated account of his exploits, the quarrels and reconciliations with Mistress Quickly, his portly flirtation with the priceless Doll Tearsheet, his witty and victorious dialogue with Judge Gascoigne, the incredible recruit-ment scene, the highly amusing dinner with Shallow interrupted by the bells of Oxford ("We have heard the chimes at midnight, Master Shallow"), the unexpected anxiety before the battle which sends the old sinner back to the language of his childhood ("I would it were bed-time, Hal, and all well'), through these and another dozen events, his ready wit, his verbal facility and the inexhaustible vitality of his character bring him – on the wave-tops of our affection – always victorious. One can well under-stand why the young Prince of Wales is unable to detach himself from his company.

Faithful to his dictum, Falstaff has not only wit for himself but stimulates wit in those near him. Mistress Quickly, Doll Tearsheet, Pistol, Bardolph, Poins and the Prince himself are perfect comic characters, a worthy chorus of ungirt nymphs and rascally tritons around this most agile whale.

The naturalness with which Shakespeare moves from very beautiful cosmic blank verse to highly adorned and intricate prose would be unrivalled were it not for a similar miracle occurring in a different key in *Hamlet*...

There remains one final point to mention – the Prince's betrayal of his incomparable old friend. But the matter is too painful for us to dwell on; even Shakespeare thought so and dispatched it in four words. In justification – from an artistic point of view – of an event which constitutes the blackest page of English history (which is saying a good deal), we should note its significance in bringing for the first time to the stage the famous British hypocrisy...

A very old and authoritative tradition claims that Shakespeare wrote *The Merry Wives of Windsor* in two weeks on the orders of

Queen Elizabeth, who 'wanted to see Falstaff in love'. If so, Elizabeth was disobeyed. *The Merry Wives* contains a character called Sir John Falstaff who, besides the name, has the age, the paunch and the hangers-on of our unforgettable friend, but with the true Falstaff he has really nothing in common at all.

Who could imagine the real Sir John being made fun of by three gossips, mocked, humiliated and dropped in the Thames with the dirty washing? In any case, if they had had the real Falstaff before them, each of the three ladies would have gone crazy about him, as we all do.

I own that of all the characters in this play the one who pleases me least is Falstaff: he is too foolish, too naive, too little like the real man. The poet had made the latter die so well, in the arms of that Mrs Quickly who now teases him, that he could not bring himself to create an identical twin.[1]

Subterranean Love: Measure for Measure

As Shakespeare says in this 144th sonnet, and as Josephine Baker reaffirms in her well-known song, each of us has "two loves". Both are genuine: one official, declared, conjugal, legal, admissible and conventional; the other secret, sinful, adulterine, illicit, clandestine and shocking. Thus Louis XV had as his mistress the beautiful, elegant and intellectual Madame de Pompadour (who was not exactly lawful but was certainly official); yet he also dallied with the young nymphs who were produced for him in the Parc aux Cerfs. Others have a public harem in which their favourites are Bartók, Brahms, Mozart and Wagner; but they also swoon under the caresses of *The Merry Widow*. Chateaubriand admired Béranger, while Baudelaire read Paul de Kock in secret. And all of them were within their rights.

[1] In his libretto for Verdi's *Falstaff* (based on *The Merry Wives*), Arrigo Boito "improved" the protagonist by adding passages from *King Henry IV*, but Lampedusa was not impressed. He strongly objected to the manhandling of Shakespeare for operatic purposes. (See below pp. 124ff.)

I also belong to this illustrious band. My (intellectual) wife is *Hamlet*; and my mistresses, whom I maintain publicly with mink coats, smart cars and rubies from Bulgari, are Cordelia, Desdemona, Lady Macbeth and Sir John. But in a small apartment in the suburbs I have a kept woman whom everyone else thinks is rather plain, a seamstress who is satisfied with a small car, a coat of rabbit fur and some cheap jewellery. And when I am with her, Hamlet seems to me a little ineffectual, Cordelia a little cold, Desdemona a bit of a goose, Lady Macbeth rather quick with her fingers, and Sir John, well, perhaps just a little too paunchy. My subterranean love is *Measure for Measure*.

If someone told me that all the works of Shakespeare must perish except one that I could save, I would first try to kill the monster who had made the suggestion. If I failed, I would then try to kill myself. And if I could not manage even this, well then, eventually, I would choose *Measure for Measure*.

Superb, indefinable poem and great, unclassifiable work of theatre, it is too tragic for comedy and too ironic for tragedy, a play in which the most beautiful lines of poetry alternate with the harshest and most "haunted" prose. Like the Pietà Rondanini which it resembles, the work displays in its rugged awkwardness dazzling signs of the most transcendental genius.

First of all the subject matter. In that unreal Vienna which bears so strange a resemblance to the Vienna of *The Third Man* (or not so strange because Graham Greene was the right person to grasp the atmosphere of *Measure for Measure*), the most abominable events unfold under the aegis of the most rigorous morality. The honour of young girls and the heads of both innocent and guilty are traded like shares in the Stock Exchange. Pimps and procurers explain their motives with the most golden and moving words. Guardians of public morality (men of the highest decency of course) immerse themselves in corruption, profit from it and increase it. "Promising young men" implore their sisters from convents to prostitute themselves to save their skins. In the dungeons an exhibition of dignity is given by a man condemned to death, a man, moreover, who is not a brute but someone capable of setting an example to respectable people. And away from this dismal prison which encompasses the whole city, in a garden on the outskirts a young man sings at dawn the most beautiful song that exists, a song of love betrayed.

But the reader knows that it will all turn out fine, that the virtuous Duke is only pretending to be absent and that in the fifth act he will return to put everything right according to morality and justice: 'measure for measure'. Yet in fact the old Duke returns and sanctions all the evil that has been done; he legitimises it, indeed he even extols it. He rewards the guilty and reproves the just. Then the curtain falls. "Measure for measure". An epigraph for the play could be the *italianissimo* (as Mussolini would say) and seldom appreciated saying, '*Andate a farvi benedire*'.[1]

And now the ambience. Shakespeare's cities are always open and friendly. The Verona of *Romeo and Juliet*, the Windsor of *The Merry Wives*, the Messina of *Much Ado about Nothing*, even the Troy of *Troilus*, are open, sunny and welcoming, at least as far as the buildings are concerned. The only nightmare up till now has been the Castle of Elsinore. But in *Measure for Measure* Evil has corrupted even the very stones. I don't know what makes me see it, but I picture that Vienna as half demolished, its walls corroded from leprosy (there are details but they are almost imperceptible), people wandering around the streets as in times of great disaster. It seems like a painting by Monsù Desiderio. And I had this sensation twenty-five years before *The Third Man* was made. A ghostly city of brothels, prisons and attics, where forsaken women weep.

Opera and Othello

Just as there are seven wonders of the world (and seven deadly sins), so there are, in my opinion, seven supreme Shakespearian

---

[1] Literally 'Go and get blessed', but the real meaning is quite the opposite and might politely be rendered, 'Go and jump in the lake'.

summits: *Henry IV, Hamlet, Measure for Measure, Othello, King Lear, Macbeth* and *Antony and Cleopatra*. . .

Othello (which is the least of the four tragedies, if we want to play the feeble game of guessing the weight of dinosaurs) has had the misfortune to fall victim to two misunderstandings – and for the Italians three. Firstly it is afflicted with a racial angle caused by the bad English translation of Italian stories used by Shakespeare. Cinzio's *Il Moro di Venezia* is not in fact a Moor but a Signor Moro, a very common surname (like Moroni and Moretti) in the Bergamo region. Lorry drivers from Lombardy, Piedmont and the Veneto still shout *"Ciao bella mora"* at any non-blond girl they come across. And if the unknown English translator had witnessed one of these encounters on the motorway, the play would have become rather more moving and the character of Desdemona rather less unusual. But nothing can be done about it now. Shakespeare swallowed the literary falsehood and from the very beginning (to be precise, line 67 of Act I, Scene 1) Othello is portrayed as "the thick lips".

The second misunderstanding is more serious. Literary critics are seldom functionaries of the state, and career officials are certainly never literary critics. Thus nobody has realised that Iago, although a very bad sort, is not Satan, a being who loves Evil for its own sake. He is simply an official who has been passed over for promotion, and to what state envy and bitterness can reduce an individual placed in this position can easily be understood in a quarter of an hour spent at a regimental mess after the Official Gazette has arrived with this unhappy news in print. In *Othello*, as in the rest of Shakespeare's works, there are no symbolic characters: there are simply a number of men and women who suffer, struggle and die, like the rest of us.

The third misunderstanding, as I have said, is specifically Italian and is connected to the second. For ninety-nine Italians out of a hundred, Othello is the name borne by a tenor for three hours on the stage. The Moor's name is associated with those of singers such as Tamagno and Marconi much more often than with that of

Shakespeare. Thus it is to Boito's libretto that we must turn to understand the view of the above average Italian.

This libretto has had much greater literary stamina than almost all the others used by Verdi. That goes without saying but does not prevent it from being fundamentally wrong, for it first mutilates and then deforms the whole play. It completely mutilates the first act in which Shakespeare (who was a more acute gentleman than Boito) prepares all the circumstances from which the tragedy unfolds, it mutilates the crucial scenes of Iago's jealousy and above all it omits Brabantio's warning which does so much to stimulate Othello's anger, "She has deceiv'd her father, and may thee".

Boito, who was the quintessence of romanticism, was delighted to abandon himself entirely to the hypothesis of Iago-Satan... And since he found nothing in Shakespeare's text which could justify such an apocalyptic vision of Iago's character, he set himself to invent this Satan and produced the famous "Credo" which is as unShakespearian, as unlike Iago – and as unlifelike – as a romantic fifty years after his time could conceive.

Such is the power exerted by operatic melodrama on Italian heartstrings that nowadays even Shakespeare's play is performed in our country without its first act, and the actors, unable to yell "I believe in a cruel god" to the audience, try to give an equivalent impression by means of satanic leers and monstrous disguises. When I went to see Orson Welles's *Othello*, I heard people behind me complaining that the director had added his own beginning to the film by inserting the Venetian scenes. For the Italians the tragedy *Othello* has been killed by the opera *Otello*.

The truth is that Iago is nothing but a second-rate malefactor, similar to dozens one finds in every type of organisation, public and private, the sort of people who write anonymous letters to superiors who have not promoted them. His wickedness is on such a parsimonious scale that he does not expect (or intend) blood to flow nor the great calamity to take place. As he puts it, he simply wants to "untune" – to destroy – the harmony existing between Othello and Desdemona. The tragedy is entirely caused by Othello's temperament, by the ease with which he becomes totally unbalanced. He is the tragic figure. Iago is merely the contemptible fuse which explodes the mine.

Othello is more or less the only Shakespearian tragedy which does not contain a comic role. Why is this? Because the comic part is assigned to "the Satan". Shakespeare was so unfrightened of Iago that he did not hesitate to give him many humorous lines. In making a list of Shakespeare's lively, witty and mordant characters, it would be unfair to neglect Iago, who in a good half of what he says resembles Benedick. His humour, of course, is bitter, saturnine and low-level.

It would be too long (and unnecessary besides) to recall the innumerable lines of fine poetry. But I would feel guilty if I failed to point out the whole of the fifth act, dense with foreboding and agonising to listen to if well performed. Othello's death would be the most magnificent of such Shakespearian scenes if it had not been preceded by the death of Hamlet, and if some months later the playwright had not devised the scornful and voluptuous end of Cleopatra.

I have never heard whether *Othello* has been performed in modern dress. Yet it is the Shakespearian play that would most lend itself to a production of this type. Indeed it would gain from mutation into a sordid intrigue in a colonial garrison – which is essentially what it is.

Opera Mania: A Digression

Macbeth has also been transformed into an opera but fortunately with less "success" than *Othello*, with the result that the *real* play has escaped untarnished. This reflection, however, has made my accumulated hatred of opera boil once more within me. The lines I dedicated to the subject when discussing *Othello* have only slightly relieved my spleen. There is still much to come, and I must vent it now or else I shall be unable to sleep.

I know nothing about music. People tell me that among the

Italian operas of the nineteenth century there are some compara-
tive masterpieces, and I'm ready to believe them. Here I only
want to consider opera in Italy as a cultural phenomenon or, to be
more precise, as an educational phenomenon.

From this point of view, it seems to me that the blossoming of
opera, the extraordinary favour it has found in Italy, and the
longevity of that favour, form one of the most sinister
phenomena to be found in the history of any culture.

The infection began immediately after the Napoleonic wars
and spread with giant steps. For more than a hundred years, tens
of thousands, hundreds of thousands of Italians went to the opera,
in the great cities for eight months a year, in the lesser cities for
four months a year and in the small towns for two or three weeks
each year. And they saw tyrants slain, lovers committing suicide,
great-hearted clowns, prolific nuns and every sort of nonsense
dished out in front of them in a continual whirling of papier-
mâché boots, plaster chickens, leading ladies with blackened faces
and devils springing out of the floor making awful grimaces. All
this synthesised, without psychological passages, without development, all bare, crude, brutal and irrefutable.

This unfathomable stupidity was not considered as common
enjoyment, as an excusable distraction for illiterate layabouts; it
was passed off as Art, as real Art, and horrors! sometimes it really
was Art. The cancer absorbed all the artistic energies of the nation:
music was opera, drama was opera, painting was opera. And
other musical forms like the symphony and chamber music
languished and died: during the nineteenth century Italy lacked
all of them. The theatre, which with its slow build-ups could not
resist the waves of "*Do di petto*",[1] died also. Painters neglected
their noble canvases to throw themselves headlong into designing
the prisons of *Don Carlos* or the sacred groves of *Norma*.

When opera mania diminished after 1910, Italian intellectual
life was like a field in which locusts had spent a hundred unbroken
years. Italians had become accustomed to citing as gospel truth the

---

[1] A phrase signifying a tenor's highest notes.

lines of Francesco Maria Piave or Cammarano;[1] to thinking that
Enrico Caruso or Adelina Patti[2] were the flower of the race; and
to believing that war was like the chorus of *Norma*. The influence
of all this on the national character is before our eyes.

Art had to be easy and the music singable. Drama consisted of
sword-thrusts flavoured with musical trills. What was not simple,
violent, within the grasp equally of a professor and dustman, was
beyond the pale.

But there was worse than this. Saturated and swollen-headed
by so much noisy foolishness, the Italians sincerely believed that
they knew everything. Did they not go almost every evening that
God gave them to listen to Shakespeare, Schiller, Victor Hugo
and Goethe? Signor Gattoni from Milan or Cavaliere Pantisi
from Palermo were convinced that universal literature had been
revealed to them because they knew the above-mentioned poets
from having heard them through the notes of Verdi and Gounod.

This went on until the advent of the cinema. The whole of the
nineteenth century, the period in which the brightest cultural
"lights" were shining all over Europe, was spent by Italians in
listening frenetically and insatiably to opera. And so now we are
the nation least interested in literature that exists, fed up (or so it
seems) with opera, but unready to listen to anything else...

Macbeth

As far as one knows, Shakespeare never went to Scotland.
Rimbaud had never seen the sea when he wrote *Le Bateau ivre*.
And just as *Le Bateau ivre* gives us a most intense and precise
feeling of the ocean, so *Macbeth* gives us a wonderful picture of
rural Scotland.

This business of "feeling for landscape" which is sometimes
communicated by great *non-descriptive* writers is one of the most

[1] Two of Verdi's librettists.
[2] Respectively the most famous tenor and the most celebrated soprano around
the turn of the century.

intriguing puzzles for the passionate reader and one that would deserve a full study from somebody. It is not surprising that Chateaubriand makes us see the forests which in his day covered the United States or gives us a clear image of the Roman countryside, or that Balzac makes us live inside the Pension Vanquer. They committed themselves to description-making, using words like brushes and paints. But when Dostoyevsky in *The Brothers Karamazov*, Verga in *I Malavoglia*, or Shakespeare in *Measure for Measure*, *The Merchant of Venice*, *Antony and Cleopatra* and *Macbeth*, portray a landscape without having written a line of description, we are left dumbfounded. There can only be two possible explanations for this: either it is my personal illusion, in which case it is pointless to go on discussing it; or there are details, chopped up finely, reduced to the state of impalpable dust and arranged with such mastery regarding characters and events as to multiply their effect many times over and together form an impression of the landscape.

Although Tolstoy was not a great "describer" either, he also conjured up incomparable images and used to say that the most beautiful and complete impression of the Russian plain in winter could be given by the phrase, "a wooden bridge over a frozen stream, crossed by two boots walking alone". This gives a vague idea of the method I am alluding to.

In *Macbeth* the Scottish countryside (among many other things) is fully revealed. This landscape, which is somewhat similar to our Alpine scenery, with its red and purple moors, almost treeless, and the ochre-coloured hills overhanging a frothy greenish sea; the grey squat towns of slate and mist (beautiful) which without transition into suburbs open straight out into the most deserted countryside; this light which is nearly perpetual but never sparkling in summer and which in winter is almost (though not completely) absent; this weird spectral landscape, charged with sorcery, animated (in a manner of speaking) by folk who talk so low they seem almost dumb; among them, though, if one is lucky, one will meet the most beautiful girls of Europe (emerald eyes in faces of milk and roses); this unforgettable, fascinating countryside which I had known already from *Macbeth* and which caused me no surprise when I first saw and recognised it.

Apart from some opening lines by Baudelaire and in one instance by Milton, there is no beginning in the literature known to me which is more dramatic or significant than *Macbeth*. And I do not only mean the witches (although they form the most convincing introduction of the supernatural to any play I know) but also the King's encounter with the wounded soldier, the incomparable account of the battle followed by those moving fragments of verse, and all the scenes which follow until the arrival at Macbeth's castle.

With a single wingbeat the eagle has soared into his sky of clouds and tempests.

Macbeth seems to me technically the most perfect of Shakespeare's plays. But this technique is instantly lost in an inexorable furnace of images so intense that they could live alone, detached from their context. Blake's remarkable watercolours, which have nothing in common with *Macbeth* except that they are extraordinary embodiments of the play's images, are a proof of it. Another is that Baudelaire was inspired by one of them – as he was in other cases by paintings – to write one of his most turbulent poems.

This extraordinary "vein", which for length and homogeneity of inspiration has no equivalent elsewhere, not even in the rest of Shakespeare, is maintained without difficulty until the end, until the last despairing cry of the criminal King. A series of scenes of denser poetry, of more compressed meaning, does not exist. It is enough to recall (apart from the incomparable beginning) the arrival at Macbeth's castle, Lady Macbeth's welcome, the scenes of murder, Banquo's death and the banquet, the striking expressions of widespread indignation, the madness of Lady Macbeth, her husband's truly cruel words on her death, and then the final scenes, to convince oneself that, as far as man is able, here he has created the perfect work.

II

Englishness

Isaak Walton

In London there is a street, St James's, which is almost entirely occupied by luxury shops for men. Ties, shoes, polo sticks and golf clubs adorn the windows of minute shops in which the quality of the articles for sale has been examined with the scrupulous care of a poet examining the lyrics which might adorn his collection. The finest shot-guns for every sort of quarry from a thrush to an elephant; every type of cartridge from the lightest for killing a bird without damaging its plumage to the most powerful for shooting dead a furious rhinoceros charging at you. Tobacco of every sort and from every country, from our own coarse "Tuscan" to certain cigars from the Philippines which smell of pineapples, Turkish cigarettes as well as Egyptian, Armenian, Afghan, Russian, Indo-Chinese, Peruvian and Australian; cigarettes whose tobacco has soaked in the oil of roses and cigarettes which after manufacture have lain for a year in the same vaults as dried cod; cigarettes with saffron, with cinnamon and with incense; cigarettes red, black and yellow; cigarettes flavoured with whisky and cigarettes flavoured with patchouli. Briar pipes, meerschaum pipes, pipes of amber and ivory, old and new, smooth and carved, rounded, cubic, in the shape of a tomato or a pyramid, straight pipes, pipes curving downwards and pipes curving up, mouthpieces of every sort from those of Manilla leaf which make the smoke cold to those dug from bones of the dead which make the soul frozen. Cigarette lighters working on petrol, gas, electricity and now, I suppose, nuclear energy;

lighters made of gold, silver, platinum, steel, jade and wood, functioning by means of springs, rollers, pistons and levers – plus flint from Tibet; lighters that do not go out unless there's a gale of 125 kms an hour, lighters with clocks and lighters with compasses, lighters which emit a dull rumbling in your pockets to warn you that the fuel is nearly finished. And the different types of fuel! Colourless, red, green, amaranth and yellow. Quick-lighting fuels and others with a delaying action, fuels scented with oregano, with *peau d'Espagne* and Chanel 22; and other fuels as well, particularly evil-smelling, which are useful for getting rid of bores.

There are wine shops, shops for walking-sticks and shops for dogs. All with a tone of refined elegance. Even the most self-possessed of men are bemused. The prices are in guineas.

But there are also shops for fishing tackle, for the noble and combative sport of angling (even tunny fish are caught this way) much practised in the seas, rivers, lakes, streams and brooks of England. These shops are overflowing from inside with hooks, rods, bait, lines, barrels and whatever man has ever designed for deceiving and destroying these innocent creatures. But the window, chastely draped with ivory-coloured velvet, exhibits only one book, a slender little volume bound in green leather: *The Compleat Angler* by Isaak Walton (finally we have reached it).

Isaak Walton (1593–1683) is at the same time one of the most solid "classic" writers in English literature and one of those still read in our own times. In his ninety years he produced only two slim books, about six hundred pages all told; but he owes his fame and constant popularity to the fact that he is the most English of the English: the model Englishman. (Besides being an excellent stylist.)

First of all he was "a scholar and a sportsman": one of his books is about fishing, the other is made up of nine brief biographies of famous men whom he knew (what he meant by "knowing" people we will see shortly). A duplicity of talents which is an indispensable requirement in England, a country in which a student, let's say from Cambridge, who excels in the composition of Greek verses is morally disqualified if, to these humanistic exploits, he does not add equivalent feats of rowing and boxing.

Walton had great talent in both fields. (Over Milton hangs an unexpressed, perhaps unconscious shadow, because to his repeated academic triumphs in ancient languages there was no corresponding success in "games".)

Apart from this, *The Compleat Angler* is a book full of flavour and humour. With the most detailed instructions on the ways of preparing bait and shortening rods, are mixed the most delightful descriptions of rivers and lakes; types of amateur and professional fishermen are delineated with the most good-humoured benevolence; the ample drinking in welcoming taverns after the fishing is narrated with a humour not unworthy of Shakespeare or Dickens; and the wisest (let us also say the most high-minded) advice about "fair play", of fair-mindedness towards rival anglers and towards the fish themselves (who must be allowed to "struggle" at their leisure) – all this is dispensed with an unexpected solemnity which makes one understand how close these things are to the good Walton's heart. This subject matter has produced the most delightful, most "Anglican" style that one can imagine: everything in "understatements", in half-tones, like a watercolour by Rowley. One needs to have a well-trained palate to appreciate how many subtle ingredients have been put into this sauce which complements that taste for shade shared by the trout and salmon of the lakes.

Very similar is the attitude Walton adopts in his "Lives". Instead of tench and carp he is dealing with men, truly illustrious men such as Donne and Herbert. But that is of no importance to Walton. For him they are not great poets but "gentlemen and friends" which is much more important. The biography of Donne discusses only his ecclesiastical life and his sermons; the fact that he was one of the greatest English lyric poets is not even mentioned. The life of Herbert describes at fascinating length how he helped a carter drag his cart out of the mud and how many pairs of shoes he distributed to the poor in his parish. Walton does not know (or pretends not to know) that Herbert was one of the greatest religious poets of his time.

In short Walton is the anti–Plutarch. Delightful Englishism, faithful mirror of that extraordinary country in which one can spend weeks in daily contact with an old gentleman before realising that he is an illustrious admiral or (as happened to me with Lord Haldane) a former Viceroy of India.[1]

Walton, one must understand, is not Shakespeare nor Donne nor Milton. There is nothing one can compare (in intensity) with Dickens or Browning. But if one wishes to know "the Englishman" in a pure state it is better to know him and ignore the others.

(Neither Hitler nor Mussolini had read him.)

Samuel Johnson

I have entitled this part of the course the "Age of Johnson". This is not a title which I myself have invented but the one which is generally given to this period. Now I must explain to you why Johnson deserves this honour, and that is not easy. Like many things in England, the country least governed by logic, it has to be perceived by intuition. Every civilised Englishman has known it, one might say, from birth. I have succeeded in understanding it only after much effort, and I hope I can succeed in making you understand it as well. I will begin by saying that the definition is correct, doubly correct and perhaps triply so. The first reason is intrinsic to Johnson himself; the other two are extrinsic and I will explain them afterwards. I will add that it is important to understand the reasons for Johnson's great fame because *Johnson is England* and to understand him is to take a short cut to understanding his country.

Johnson was a man of the highest learning, of that degree of learning that in any other country would have forced him to

---

[1] Haldane was never Viceroy of India. Lampedusa may have been confusing him with Lord Hardinge of Penshurst.

espouse a philosophy. Johnson's philosophy does not exist. He was a pure empiricist. First point.

Johnson's learning was exclusively classical or English. Other countries did not exist for him, not because of any nationalist zeal (it was he who proclaimed that "patriotism is the last refuge of a scoundrel") but because of his absolute and innate inability to comprehend anything other than the English style. Second point.

He did not belong to any particular sect and had not set foot in a church "since my mother dragged me there by my ear". Yet every evening before going to sleep and every morning he knelt in his nightshirt beside his bed and said his prayers. And he used to justify his behaviour by referring to such and such a passage from the Bible. Johnson was a religious man. Third point.

He was full of humour, a choleric, uncompromising, sometimes coarse humour, like Swift. Fourth point. Johnson was born in Lichfield, a grim industrial town in the Midlands, and lived for fifty years in Cheapside, right in the centre of the City of London which in his time was the heart of the already immense capital. But each Sunday he took himself out into the country, had a picnic on the grass and returned home with a bunch of wild flowers. Every Englishman, like him, is a countryman in exile, even if he lives in the middle of square kilometres of buildings. Fifth point.

When he was working for a publisher on his *Lives of the Poets*, he refused to return the proofs (preferring instead to pay a heavy forfeit) before receiving from the provinces some insignificant information about the life of an obscure poet. Another time he got up in the middle of the night to go to the printing press to correct the punctuation of an article. The scruples not so much of righteousness but of a man who cares about his profession. Sixth point.

Each morning at five o'clock Johnson had a cold bath and he also changed his shirt every day. But his shoes were seldom polished and he often had dirty nails: the content is more important than the appearance. Seventh point.

One evening he was assaulted by thieves who robbed him and

beat him up to such an extent that he lost three teeth and had two ribs broken. To the friends who visited him he said he was surprised by so much concern because all that had happened was a lively exchange of opinions. (Any one of us [Sicilians] would have cried, "They have killed me!") On another occasion he was received by the King who in recognition of his talents gave him a snuffbox studded with diamonds. At the coffee-house the following morning he said that the King had been very kind: "He has given me the means to take snuff." *Understatement*. Eighth point.

I could continue but it would be pointless. It is the fusion, the mutual animation of these and many other English characteristics that formed the character of Johnson. One example, ten examples, a hundred examples are not enough unless one grasps the astonishing fact that these national peculiarities all met in one man who was, for other reasons, so remarkable. Dante, to give a different case, was a good example of "the Italian". He possessed many of the characteristics that we all have: the cult of form, figurative language, the factiousness, the poverty, the sense of political exile. Imagine that we now knew for certain that he had also been a gossip, a womaniser and a double-crosser: he would no longer be Signor Dante Alighieri, he would be Italy. Similarly, our man of letters is no longer Dr Samuel Johnson but Mr John Bull.

Many people before him had possessed two or three or ten of these English peculiarities. No-one either before or after has possessed all of them, or at least no-one that we know of. And here we arrive at an extrinsic reason for Johnson's fame. Living in England at that time was James Boswell, a strange type of Scotsman, partly a man of letters and partly one of that extraordinary regiment of adventurers which invaded Europe at the end of the eighteenth century (and to which Italy contributed with its Goranis, Casanovas and Cagliostros). This curious fellow regarded Johnson with limitless devotion. He saw him every day and for several hours; on leaving, he noted down in great detail what Johnson had said and done. And after his death, Boswell published his biography, an enormous work, part monumental pyramid and part washerwoman's gossip, which combine to make it the finest biography ever written. I feel justified in calling it a pyramid because inside Johnson is guarded like one of those Egyptian mummies to which people wanted to grant all the gifts of life.

Boswell himself stands aside and gives us the pleasure of hearing Johnson's voice as if it were a gramophone recording, of understanding his sarcasm, of appreciating the wisdom of his judgments. And around him is the picturesque crowd of contemporary writers, some haughty, others voracious, all subjected to the scowl of the Master. This is the "pyramidal side". On the "laundry side" we are told about the subject's personal habits, his whims, his gastronomic tastes and his clothes with such a mass of detail that his living presence becomes almost overpowering. Boswell's *Life of Johnson* is one of the key books in English literature. Johnson had the extraordinary good fortune not only to incarnate his own country but also to be the 'least...dead' of men.

To this should be added the second extrinsic reason: the admirable portrait painted by Reynolds which shows him alive and pulsating in all his ugliness, with his warts and those serious eyes that resemble an intelligent dog's.

Recently Boswell's diaries, written before he met Johnson, have been discovered and published. These are also of total sincerity and give us in a couple of volumes a picture of the epoch that otherwise one could obtain only through studying hundreds of documents. It used to be said that Boswell without Johnson would have been nothing. Perhaps it was true. In any case Johnson without Boswell would have been very much less than he is now.

"But," you will say, "what has this blessed man written to deserve such authority in his lifetime and such a reputation after his death? We had never heard of him before."

He wrote a good deal: little of great value though several things are useful. Above all he excelled in the type of criticism which was in those days the most immediate and effective: spoken criticism. Socrates never wrote a thing. But he talked, he taught and he influenced a restricted circle of people which contained the seeds of the human future.

Johnson's principal works are *A Dictionary of the English Language* (1755) and *Lives of the Poets*. Although compiled a hundred years before them, the Dictionary is the equivalent of our Tommaseo or the French Littré, and was the first to use passages from great writers to clarify the meaning of words. In it he demonstrates that he was not only a great philologist but also a skilled writer, capable of grasping different nuances in the meaning of words. Naturally since then the English language has changed a good deal, but for those words that were contemporary or preceded him, Johnson remains valuable. [In] *Lives of the Poets* ... Johnson's honesty shines through every page: his judgments are always just except in the case of Milton whom he detested for political reasons.

Apart from these two colossal works, Johnson wrote an account of a visit to Scotland, numerous fine essays and a sort of philosophical novella which has as its setting Abyssinia (for which he always had a curious esteem), *Rasselas*, which is delightful and which I still have. He also wrote some verses in the manner of Boileau: a satirical poem "London" and the moralistic "The Vanity of Human Wishes", which are not bad. He wrote, too, a great many critical works among the most notable of which are a defence of the old English drama and an attack on Aristotelian unity, which was plagiarised by French Romantics (a euphemism so as not to mention Victor Hugo) when, sixty years later, they wished to create "the new theatre".

G. K. Chesterton

Before discussing G. K. Chesterton it may be useful to say something about English Catholic writers.

There is a great difference between Italian Catholic writers and those in England (or to tell the truth in any other country). The Italian writer who openly professes himself a Catholic is always a "flabby" writer. But the English (or French or German or American) writer who fights for the Catholic Church is invariably a "tough" writer. This arises from the fact that in England, Germany and the United States Catholicism is a minority religion in opposition to other confessions and requires resolution, aggression and courage to affirm and maintain it. In France too, Catholicism is in a minority with respect not to other forms of religion but to various shades of unbelief. In France, therefore, the same virtues also are needed among the faithful and among those writers who wish to expound their convictions. This is the cause of that magnificent flowering of French Catholic writers over the last century, a flowering which began with Maistre and Bonald (the masters) and has given us Lamennais, Montalembert, Veuillot, Bloy and Péguy before we come to our contemporaries Bernanos, Mauriac and Claudel – all of them more or less great writers, all at any rate combative scribes with spurs and sharp swords. We are a long way from our own Fogazzaro, Salvadori and Fausto Maria Martini, in whose works one notices not the incense of the church but the odour of the sacristy, which is less good. Exceptions consist of Father Bresciani, whom no-one reads although he was a great man, and our contemporaries Papini and Giuliotti, in whose works, however, the vehemence is too often rhetorical and seems more concerned with the appearance of Catholicism than with its soul.

The Italians are too unbelieving even to be anti-Catholics. And, one has to ask, against whom should our Catholic thinkers draw their swords? Maistre sallied forth as a counterweight to Voltaire, and Veuillot would not have existed without Renan. Against whom among us could the Catholics fight – against Podrecca? It's not worth it. The struggle against Giovanni Gentile could not take place because he was not simply anti-religious but also a Fascist. And so the intellectual Catholic ambience continues to exist in a temperature redolent of tepid soup, which promotes the germination of microbes but not of polemicists.

(In spite of the temperature and my good intentions, my verbosity has got out of control.)

We must not concern ourselves with the French or the Italians, however, but with the English. With us Catholicism, besides being the church of ninety-seven per cent of the population, stems from a period of plainly unproductive dominance. Thus the Italian Catholic is full of unconscious remorse and always seems to be apologising for being one. In England the Catholics are five per cent of the population and issue from a long period of persecution, bloody to begin with, over property and politics later on, and oppressive always, which places them in the advantageous position of being the accusers. Add to this the fact that, from contact with other, more austere faiths, English Catholicism abandoned almost all the less noble manifestations and slipped away from the more abstruse dogmatic definitions. And furthermore, if you consider that the long centuries of persecution removed the lukewarm and the Catholics "out of habit", you will realise that being an English Catholic is very different, indeed almost opposite, to being an Italian one. The priesthood is sparse but magnificent, and under vestments very similar to those worn by the Anglican clergy, possesses authentic Christian virtues. And the writers follow the same general directions.

I will not speak to you of Cardinal Newman, an excellent writer but rather remote in time, nor of Hopkins who needs a separate discussion and whose importance in any case is exclusively literary. I am going to talk only of Chesterton and of the small but valiant group which formed under him and which after his death continues to promote his ideas.

Chesterton was a poet of merit in his non-poetical fashion, and a novelist and storyteller of exceptional value. But above all he was, as a poet, a novelist and a writer of essays and articles, a most valiant and indefatigable polemicist.

To formal Catholicism he arrived late, fully converting not many years before his death. But he had always polemicised on behalf of what he cared deeply about and which he identified with

Catholicism: respect for tradition, defence of human individualism threatened by socialism, defence of charity in its Catholic sense against any form of hypocritical beneficence and state insurance. His secondary adversaries were "prohibitionists" and colonialists.

The cataloguing of his targets is clearly sufficient to make you understand in whom his enemy was incarnated – George Bernard Shaw. It was a great epoch between 1910 and 1930 when these two polemical super-champions fought each other in the press in front of the English public which, with its sporting customs, impartially applauded the best hits from whichever side they came.

Faithful to English traditions, the two adversaries were close friends and, when one of them thought up a witty remark which he could not make use of, it seems that he communicated it by telephone to the other so that his rival could use it and prevent its being lost. "Fair Play".

Let's begin with the poems, which are among the most amusing in existence. Written in metres either taken from ancient ballads or else borrowed from Kipling, they form a succession of the best "jokes" ever written in verse or prose. It would be pointless to list all the collections of the poems. The best are *The Ballad of the White Horse* and *Wine, Water and Song*, which among others contains those poems – some of his funniest – included in the novel *The Flying Inn*. In a more elevated style *The Ballad of St Barbara* and in particular *Lepanto* at times reach the heights of true poetry.

Chesterton's novels and stories are numerous and in many cases worthless from an artistic point of view – if one subtracts their polemical impetuosity which is always remarkable. Among the best I would put *Manalive*, *The Ball and the Cross*, and *The Napoleon of Notting Hill*. Among the worst are *The Flying Inn* although it contains the author's most original lyrics. But let me make it clear that, good or bad, all are highly amusing and full of brio, featuring caricatures of real or imaginary people drawn with diabolical cunning.

But Chesterton's best fictional works are *The Man Who Was Thursday* and the series of Father Brown stories. The first (like almost all of Chesterton's stories) resembles a *conte philosophique* of Voltaire but set in a worldly ambience with a very different target. In it the author intended to deride modern science and the philosophy on which it is based, which ends by identifying Evil with Good. There are not two more different styles than those of Chesterton and Voltaire, the latter's as lean and aerial as the former's is crowded and fattened with words from the vernacular. But apart from the extreme maliciousness common to both, they also each possess the secret of rapid movement which allows no time for reflection and the ability to embody the most abstract philosophical opinions in living characters.

The continuous good humour, the aptitude for caricature, and the sudden phrases that reveal unexpected theological depths, make this short novel a masterpiece.

Almost all the detective stories of Father Brown are also masterpieces. Indeed one can say that this Father Brown, together with Sherlock Holmes, is the only character from a detective story who achieves the status of art. He is the priest-detective who is searching not so much for crime as for sin, and sometimes he finds more "sin" in the victim than in the criminal. Chesterton also succeeded in depicting an "ambience" around Father Brown which is far removed from that existing (or rather, not existing) in other detective stories. Except when Flambeau, the unpleasant repentant criminal, appears, all these stories end with the discovery not only of the criminal but, more importantly, of a subtle psychological truth.

As good Italians who desire "serious" literature so as to be able to lead an unserious life more comfortably, you will naturally curl up your nose. But you are wrong. A good dose of Chestertonian reading will do you a lot of good.

The greater part of Chesterton's work, however, is found outside both poetry and fiction. There are dozens of collections of articles, and at least a dozen volumes of... I don't know what to call them – "theoretical works" let's say. The most remarkable of these is *Orthodoxy*, which is quite his finest work. It is a long essay on orthodoxy, not in its purely religious sense but also on the orthodoxy of life, on what we call "public morality". The subject matter may seem a little grey, but open the volume at any page and you will remain captivated to the end. The author's paradoxical spirit shows us the tritest truths turned on their heads so that they appear to us as original. By means of paradoxes, witticisms and outbursts of poetry, the argument in favour of traditional morality, of the old way of living, and of a simplicity of existence, clearly emerges. And deep down the old England has listened to it.

With the passing of the years, Chesterton's output declined in quality. *Heretics* is still good though plainly inferior to *Orthodoxy*, but his biography of St Francis ("biography" in so far as an impetuous soul like his could understand it) and his account of a journey in the United States are distinctly bad, as are his last stories, *The Club of Queer Trades*, *The Return of Don Quixote*, *The Man Who Knew Too Much*. Besides these, there are numerous collections of articles which follow the same path. The earliest are excellent but the last are worse than mediocre and suffer from a superfluous and tiresome accumulation of witticisms.

But as a whole Chesterton's work is extremely interesting, amusing and nourishing. A knowledge of it, even if limited to the four or five best works, is indispensable for anyone who does not wish to think that the positivism, the materialism and the witty but arid mentality of Shaw are uncontested in England...

III

Prejudice and Predilection

Keats among the Angels

I am a person who is very often alone. Of the sixteen hours of daily wakefulness, at least ten are spent in solitude. And being unable, after all, to read the whole time, I amuse myself by constructing literary theories... such as my theory of the "angels".

From time to time there appear on this earth beings whose existence radiates a superhuman light. But to belong to this very restricted elite, genius alone is not sufficient. Neither Shakespeare nor Dante nor Michelangelo nor Baudelaire are among the angels. Maybe they are gods but they are not angels.

To be included among their number it is necessary to die very young or to cease all activity at an early age. One condition, it goes without saying, is that their work is of supreme value, while another is that their presence is short and brilliant, so that they leave us grey mortals with the sensation that they are superhuman visitors who watched us for an instant and then returned to the heavens, bequeathing us gifts of divine quality and also a bitter regret at the fleetingness of the apparition.

Among the "angels" I place Raphael and Masaccio, Mozart and Hölderlin, Rimbaud and Maurice de Guérin, Shelley,

Marlowe and Keats (as you can see, the "angels"' ethics do not concern me). Rupert Brooke and Novalis have just missed promotion to this group, along with Giorgione and Van Gogh. Péguy had the right qualifications to become an angel except that he died too late; Sergio Corazzini died at the right time but did not have sufficient talent. "Women angels" abound, but they are a very different species.

The first named are indisputably the true "angels". In this list, shining with joy and for us tears, the supreme place goes to John Keats. Of all of them, he alone is absolutely pure. I know it is not their fault, but a few spots of mud stain the wings of Marlowe and Shelley. Rimbaud is undoubtedly an angel but, like Marlowe, one is not sure if he comes from above or from below. Raphael's lechery, Hölderlin's madness, Masaccio's bad temper and Mozart's wife are faint blemishes on the whiteness of their clothing. But angel of the first degree, archangel, seraphim, cherubim, angel in full relief, angel of one hundred carats, angel with top-quality wings guaranteed against moths – the only one is John Keats.

Scott and Boredom

Walter Scott is one of those writers who over the years have undergone a severe devaluation. From 1810 until his death, and for several decades afterwards, he was considered both the greatest and the most enjoyable of novelists. He was translated into every language, and I have an edition of *Ivanhoe* published in Palermo in 1832. Nowadays he is read by almost nobody abroad and by very few people in England. He is invariably awarded that title [Bore] which a friend of ours gives to any writer whose work exceeds two hundred pages.

The strange thing is that this epithet is only partly deserved. The start of every novel is truly unbearable. Scott describes hair by hair, line by line, the face of every character; after that there is no ribbon of a dress or buckle of a boot left unscrutinised; and after that the castle is described with the scruple of an architect and the surrounding countryside with the pedantry of an official from the land register. And all this is done without any talent or well-chosen adjective which evokes the scene. A hundred pages go by and one is astonished that such a bore could ever, in any age, have enjoyed such a great reputation.

But by the hundreth page the worthy Scott has managed to imprint the faces and places in our memory. He has ended his function as scene-shifter and make-up artist and raised the curtain on his play.

The drama is described in masterly fashion: the psychology of the characters is solid, the action alive and rapid – just as much movement as in Dumas but with incomparably more flesh on it. Athos, Bussy d'Amboise and the Count of Monte Cristo are abstractions, geometrical figures; Guy Mannering, the Antiquary and Amy Robsart are full-blooded characters. Instead of abridging whole novels of Scott for children, as is now done, the first hundred pages should be reduced to ten and the rest left intact. Even our friend would read pages 101 to 500 and his favourite word would freeze upon his lips.

Jane Austen and the Italians

Jane Austen is one of those writers who need to be read slowly: a moment's inattention can make one overlook a crucial phrase, for her art is one of nuances and ambiguities under an apparent simplicity. Her novels are the *Maximes* of La Rochefoucauld set in motion...

Jane Austen's standing in Italy is nil. Some of her novels have indeed been translated, but no-one has paid them any attention. The reason is obvious: Jane Austen is *l'anti-melodramma*, the antithesis of opera. Disappointed at finding no daggers, no poisoned cups, none of those horribly explicit passions to which opera has accustomed it, the Italian public probably thinks that nothing happens in her novels. And that, thank goodness, is true.

Nothing does happen. And yet even an Italian reader (provided opera has not put his brain out of order) may be unable to detach himself from her pages. Through them flows a gentle existence: people fall in love without having to yell a love aria; they hate each other without deafening themselves with the *do di petto*. No-one drinks anybody's blood.

"Dear Jane". Virtuous, genteel creature that you are, the very antithesis of the operatic soprano – your genius shines with a gentle light, it doesn't dazzle with flashing blades, for yours was a world of humdrum melancholy with nothing of the tragic, a world of gaiety free of ridicule. Come, "dear Jane", come and join us awhile and exorcise the loud, overblown and superficial spirits which have delighted the common herd for a century and a half and deprived more sensitive beings of tranquil slumber.

The fausse bonhomie of Robert Burns

In England there is a public, more restricted than in France but larger than in Italy, which loves true poets. Next comes a much larger layer of people who are not very cultured but like to read obscure poets to give themselves the illusion that they understand the Eleusinian Mysteries. Below this stratum, but before reaching Guy Brothby's public, there are innumerable people, generally uncultured and with sentimental natures, who go mad about Robert Burns.

At the same time there is that entire Scottish faction which, anxiously searching for a national poet, has clung to Burns. And this faction, consisting of Scottish professors, journalists and intellectuals in general, has ended up by giving an "official" seal to that same taste for Burns possessed by his less cultured English public. Favourite alike of his low-level English admirers and of all the Scots, many of them eminent, Burns has officially become a Great Poet.

He is in fact the typical *faux bonhomme* type of writer who makes an affectation of extreme simplicity, who says he finds the English language too difficult and therefore takes refuge in the Scottish dialect. The simple lyrics, overstated and over-sentimental—the type of lyric which all the greatest poets from Shakespeare to Goethe used occasionally as a by-product of their real art—represent the summit of Burns's achievement.

His horizons are too narrow, his interests too parochial. And behind every invocation of "Auld Lang Syne", behind the maudlin elegies for the shepherdesses of Scotland, one detects a whiff of that whisky for which he maintained an immoderate devotion. A poet, in short, provincial by destination whom a lucky wind blew up to the highest peaks. In him we see what Giovanni Meli would have become had the Sicilian separatist dream been realised.

Having heard this, however, I advise you to find an anthology and read some poems of the good Robbie. I am speaking not only of Scotland but also of England when I advise you not to try wooing a girl without quoting some lines from Burns. There is a singular purity about this poet that will inebriate her to the point of banishing her every notion of personal purity. From this point of view Burns is invaluable.

Haworth and Emily Brontë

Imagine a small two-storeyed house... around which a little garden, without trees to cast shadows over its monotonous box hedges, struggles to survive. Leading from it is the immense moor, boundless and bare, yellow-dry in summer, heather-red in autumn, snow-white in winter, grass-green in spring, always one colour, always without movement and wholly deserted. The swaying curves of the surrounding hills invite sleep, or rather they would invite sleep if it was not for the hostile ruler of the place, the wind: an incessant wind which gallops freely as an open sea, which howls dark threats throughout the days and lengthy nights, and which stunts the growth of trees...

I must now speak of Emily, the passionate, brilliant, immortal and unforgettable Emily. She wrote only a few poems, short, sharp, wounded lyrics from whose spell one cannot escape. And one novel, *Wuthering Heights*, a novel such as has never been written before and never will be again. It has been compared to *King Lear*, but really Emily makes us think not of Shakespeare but of Freud, a Freud, that is, whose freedom from prejudice and whose tragic disenchantment were united to the highest and purest artistic gifts. The book consists of a dark narrative of hatred, sadism and repressed passion, told in a taut and corruscating style that emanates a savage purity through a tale of tragedy. The romantic novel has here reached its summit: the werewolves of Borel and the monsters of Godwin are nothing compared with this novel. I have specially read it just now, and the impression of hidden greatness and stabbing pain it used to give me returned more piercingly than ever. The consumptive Emily must have listened a good deal to the howling wind during her feverish nights. In this book, which belongs to the highest category of masterpieces, she descended deep, deep down into the human heart and naturally arrived in Hell.

I V

Dickens

The Cosmic Creators

All artists are creators of men, even if only of themselves. Some, however, have been given the power of creating worlds. The cosmic creators, it seems to me, include Homer, Shakespeare, Cervantes, Jane Austen, Fielding, Ariosto, Balzac, Manzoni, Tolstoy and Proust. As you will have understood, the ability to create worlds is not in itself an indication of supreme artistic talent, yet almost always one is dealing with artists of the first rank, possibly with the sole exception of Ariosto. He did indeed create a world whereas Leopardi did not, yet one would have to be blind not to see that the difference between them in the hierarchy of poets is the same as that between a cabin boy and an admiral in the hierarchy of sailors. . .

Regardless of their particular artistic gifts, the creators of worlds must have produced a vast and densely populated body of work, homogeneous in its variety and possessing the ability to live independently of its creator, illuminated by its own particular light and enriched by its own special landscape. Close your eyes and reflect: for each of the above mentioned names a precise image will appear: Ulysses and the Mediterranean sun, La Mancha sultry and implacable, the forests of Carolingian France, the salons of Paris, the snowy plains across which wolves or Frenchmen are hunted, the peaceful English parks, the "mountains rising from the water", the narrow, twisted streets of Angoulême – landscapes from the worlds of Homer, Cervantes, Ariosto, Proust, Tolstoy, Austen, Fielding, Manzoni and Balzac.

With Shakespeare one hesitates to mention a landscape because he created more than one world. . .

Dickens was one of the most distinguished creators of worlds. And his is one of the strangest. We know every field, every street and every face in it, and yet each time we must remind ourselves that we have never met anything like it, although perhaps we will see it again if we are good and go to Heaven. Dickens's kingdom is *magic realism*, a kingdom infinitely attractive but most difficult to rule. Only Kafka had one similar, but the laughter of Dickens makes his the more beautiful.

The Pickwick Papers

No other literature contains a book like *Pickwick Papers*. It is a fairy tale without the supernatural which has as its genie a warm-hearted and bespectacled old man. There is all the gaiety and appetite of Rabelais without his lasciviousness. The three hundred characters and the thirty-five inns in which they meet reveal to us the entire Dickensian world foreshortened. In his other works the author merely has to develop it, expand it and show us some other districts. But the nucleus, the core, is there in its entirety. . . One goes from delight to delight, from smile to smile, from observation to observation without a moment of boredom, dragged along by the rhythm of the dance which the author has imposed upon his tale. And when one closes the immense volume, it seems that a mere quarter of an hour has gone by. Thank goodness one can start all over again and always find new pearls. . .

Dickens's London

Dickens is London's poet. He knows the city in its fogs and hazy sunshine, in its wretched back streets where no ray of light can penetrate, in its sluggish yellow river, in its breathlessness and its excitement. He has described this London, which is more a forest of houses than a city, and transformed it with the sole object of making it more comprehensible. Some chapters of *Martin Chuzzlewit*, which describe (in the manner of great writers, with a few faint brushstrokes) the City, make one feel giddy. To whatever mean lodging house, to whatever hidden alleyway his eccentric characters have taken themselves, Dickens himself has been there.

Fortunate city which, like Paris, has won the supreme accolade, that of having every corner investigated by a genius. When the H Bomb destroys it, the city's death will be only apparent. Palermo, on the other hand, will die completely, though not Catania. Dickens's picture, moreover, is not a flat photographic reproduction but a painting in which the artist's vision has transformed reality by exaggeration (which thus becomes a synonym for art) and has illuminated its essential characteristics and the secret of its spirit. "He made London like a dream," Watts-Dunton has rightly said...

Dombey and Son

In *Dombey and Son* Dickens hits the low point of his work. The plot is forced, the characters are sham – talking puppets – and deserve to be in an opera. There are – there could not fail to be – some delightfully vivacious minor characters, but they do not manage to redeem the novel. Even the London of *Dombey and Son* is out of focus and lacking those imaginative touches to which Dickens has accustomed us. There is a small boy called Paul whose death, from a mysterious aetiological illness, is pure opera. Although it pains me to say so, his delirium, in which he asks repeatedly "What are the wild waves saying?" is worthy of Donizetti...

Dickens's Characters, Major and Minor

Dombey and Son was followed a year later by *David Copperfield*, which is certainly "the second best" of Dickens's novels and for some even the best... It contains Micawber the Immortal, the eternal optimist, the virtuous rascal, Falstaff's one brother in all literature...As for *A Tale of Two Cities*, it seems an excellent story recounted by a different writer who possesses all those virtues of reserve, literary modesty and, in short, sobriety which Dickens did not have, and which completely lacks the brio, the inspiration and the unbridled verbal imagination of the creator of Pickwick. It is like a Shakespearian comedy written by Ben Jonson. I think it's unnecessary to say which way my perifidious taste inclines...

One needs to say a word about Dickens's minor characters, by whom I mean the really minor ones who appear just once or twice. In thousands of novels by thousands of writers we will read a sentence of this type: "Commendatore Attilio Gattoni got out of the taxi at the entrance to the station and, after paying the driver, summoned a porter to carry the luggage to his compartment." In Dickens both the porter and the taxi driver are described – and described splendidly. You will know the warts on their faces, the stains on their clothes, and the polite or impolite things they will say to each other and to the Commendatore Gattoni: they will become part of the Dickensian world. This rule is always followed, even in the less successful novels, and it is this which gives the entire opus such an intense sensation of teeming life.

V

Greene and Christianity

Graham Greene is a major figure, a writer of international importance and, in my unheeded opinion, the one writer with all the qualities to occupy that place which Aldous Huxley did not know how to reach: that of the finest English novelist. . .

His warmest admirers (who are not always the most discerning of readers) are often surprised by how strongly Greene is attracted, without repugnance, to everything that is repulsive and putrid. But his is simply the Christian way. If Christ had refused to touch the lepers or talk to the Samaritan woman, the first would have stayed sick and the second would have remained a sinner. A Christian *must* be attracted to fetid carcases, as hyenas are, or Baudelaire, or the angel of the Resurrection. In Greene horror for the filthiness of the brutish, unredeemed human being is mitigated by the insuppressible resemblance to God which he finds in the most wretched delinquent; his repulsion is transformed, as he has magnificently put it, into "a forward flight" to try to wash the mud and the gore from features which are essentially divine.

Greene has gone back to the roots of Christianity and has cleansed it of all the Cardinals, the Luthers, the Archbishops of Canterbury, the Madonnas of Syracuse, the Puritans and the Jesuits, and he has found its true face, the face of Charity.

No-one claims he is a saint: perhaps *part* of his curiosity about evil comes from a wish to see it at first hand, maybe from a desire to provide himself with material for his books. But on reading him it becomes clear that the main impulse stems from a desire to plumb the depths of abasement, to comprehend the ugly reality of sin and of everything else which challenges beauty and purity. It was not only journalistic spirit which drove him to spend months in the Liberian interior... or to get himself sent to disease-ridden West Africa, or to explore other sinister parts of the earth, or to spend so many nights in London's air-raid shelters during the Blitz, of which he has left us such horrific descriptions.

It would be a mistake, however, to think of Graham Greene entirely made of austerity and wrath. He is a writer with tastes as well as convictions. His moral preoccupations do not exclude pleasure, his wit is not simply merciless satire. He knows how to be benevolent and does not possess that peculiar fear of "kindness" which is common to so many of his (and our) inferior contemporaries.

Greene wrote a number of books, particularly at the beginning of his career, for the simple aim of entertainment: all of these indeed bear the subtitle "An Entertainment". They must not be ignored, firstly because they are truly entertaining, and secondly because the author's serious side continuously shines through them: thus they help to illuminate aspects of his personality which are kept in the background of his major works...

Brighton Rock is the first of Greene's intentionally serious novels. It is the story of a crime, of its causes and moral conse-quences, a crime committed by a precocious minor who is already an inveterate criminal. What is already in Chesterton's *Father Brown* – the crime viewed as an infraction of the moral code and not only of the written law, plus compassion for the criminal together with an investigation into the possible culpability of the victim – which as I say is in Chesterton but hastily done and adorned with too many paradoxes, is here pitilessly examined, the evil dissected and the matter resolved with Christian love. It is a book which combines all the suspense of a manhunt with the subtlest of moral lessons (never expressed, thank goodness, in sermons), a book whose feverish style produces almost hallucinat-ory effects, sometimes with elements of Russian fiction which are admirably assimilated in a very different and much less tender mentality. A book which by itself would take its author to the top.

Moral and spiritual problems also dominate *The Heart of the Matter*, a story of sin and crime unfolding in the poisoned atmosphere of a British African colony. In a world of ugliness and dejection the human spirit struggles with the overbearing devil and is able in defeat to reaffirm its own eternity. In the horror of the ambience we find ourselves back among the themes of Mauriac.

But like Mauriac, Greene has been overwhelmed by moral preoccupations. And precisely because he is himself too convinced, he does not succeed in convincing us. Let it be understood, nevertheless, that this is a superior work of art.

If *The Heart of the Matter* can be debated, *The Power and the Glory* is above all criticism in its completeness as a masterpiece. I am sure you will have read it, but if you haven't yet done so, run and buy a copy even in translation. You will lose the rough and tasty language of the original, but you will find the greatness of the plot intact. Out of the most abject ambience imaginable, an ambience of vice, squalor, decay and fear, Greene has managed to create – with his drunken, lustful and yet saintly "whisky priest" – one of the most powerful figures in English literature. This priest, immersed in mortal sin, who is nevertheless the salvation of other sinners, may be the greatest ecclesiastical figure ever invented. In his soul and in those of others, maimed and brutalised, love is revealed through sin. "Hate is just a failure of the imagination." "When you saw the lines at the corners of the eyes, the shape of the mouth, how the hair grew, it was impossible to hate."

But Greene does not preach. Here he is pitiless and distant. In this work, which evokes life in its worst aspects and fear in its most terrible forms, he has also evoked mercy and reinterpreted Christianity in the terms of its original charity.

TUTORIALS ON STENDHAL

I
Introductory

All Stendhal's works are of top quality and considerable interest. Even the minor ones are impregnated with his highly original personality that irrepressibly permeates the stalest and at first sight most barren of projects. *Promenades dans Rome*, for example, is the only "travel guide" which is a literary masterpiece, while a reading of *De l'Amour* reveals a literary quality that places it well above that miscellany of anecdotes and reflections on love which it might have been, as well as those innumerable "physiologies" which were flooding the book market in those days, books so tasteless that not even Balzac's genius would have known how to react to them.

What I have said about these two books goes for all the so-called minor works which I have not mentioned, all of which have a very personal tone as well as a human and literary value.

Stendhal's two masterpieces, however, contain a further trait: many-sidedness, that is the quality of being considered from different points of view, a characteristic feature of great works which are designed in such a way as to present long and diverse intellectual perspectives from whatever point of view they are regarded.

Le Rouge et le Noir and *La Chartreuse* may be regarded as historical novels, by which I mean that they have become historical to us, as total realisations of epochs which were contemporary for their author but have become remote to us and perceptible only through art.

Balzac is what he is, but that score of novels which tries to revive the social ambience of the Restoration does not achieve the clarity of evocation reached in the five hundred pages of *Rouge et Noir* (and also in *Armance* and *Lamiel*). This book has everything: the motives, the impulses and the reactions, the cultural breadth, the creakings and confusions, the sense of a new dawn, the *couleur du temps*, of that vital crossroads of French history. Other works or memoirs of the period merely confirm (in a much more wishy-washy way) Stendhal's miraculous insight.

The same perceptiveness is displayed in *La Chartreuse* in which Italy's pre-Risorgimento period is evoked with tender irony. Together with Byron's letters and some happy flashes in the novels of Madame de Staël, *La Chartreuse* is the most important testimony of that crucial and (aesthetically) unknown period. The lack of unofficial papers is astonishing.

If, after examining the two masterpieces from an objective angle, we move a few paces, the monuments will display an entirely different perspective, a lyrical one. And I do not think the word "lyrical" unsuited to this dry and most eighteenth-century author.

In Julien Sorel Stendhal portrayed himself with his ambitious yearnings as he really was. In Fabrizio del Dongo, by contrast, he created the man he would have liked to be, a person who was noble, rich and loved, which he was not. He gave him life and shut him up in prison, a moving expression of the clarity of his insight.

Through these two characters runs Stendhal's continuous vitality, his inexhaustible curiosity, the zest for life which conditions his quest. "*Si la vie cessait d'être une recherche elle ne serait plus rien.*" This phrase from his letters characterises the endings of his two novels, which are so savagely syncopated. Here the author remorselessly destroys his protagonists: they no longer interest him nor even exist for him from the moment when, by their respective conquests of Mathilde and Clélia, they found what they were searching for, consequently stopped searching – and thus stopped being alive...

II

Stendhal's Style

Stendhal's style has been subjected to numerous observations, two types of which survive, the oldest and the most recent. The earliest is built on what he himself said: "*Mon idéal de style est celui du Code Civil.*" In his letters and diaries we frequently find examples of his contempt "*pour les phrases*" and the low esteem in which he held even the most distinguished poets.

Free of all artifice, alien to contrived phrases, hostile to intentional rhythms and miserly with adjectives, Stendhal's prose style is that of the eighteenth century with the one difference that Voltaire, for example, intended only to express reasoning while Stendhal, with the same economy of method, resolved to transmit feelings to the reader.

His talent for slimming down, discarding superfluities and sticking to the point comes close to genius. One example is well known. When Fabrizio, after numerous attempts and manoeuvres, succeeds in entering Clélia's bedroom, the consequences of this triumph are described in five words: "*Aucune résistance ne fut opposée.*" Miraculous self-control which achieves the highest artistic effect. Imagine what universes of adjectives Hugo would have used! Stendhal's sentence is surpassed only by Manzoni's famous words about Geltrude.

But there is even better. In *Le Rouge et le Noir* Stendhal was able to summarise a night of love in a semi-colon: "*La vertu de Julien fut égale à son bonheur; il faut que je descende par l'échelle dit-il à Mathilde, quand il vit l'aube du jour paraître.*"

In these instances the writer's aesthetic desire for brevity is aided by that lack of interest in his characters brought on by the "end of the quest". Once they have reached the bedrooms of Mathilde and Clélia (with all that these rooms signify besides love), Julien and Fabrizio are for Stendhal dead and useless.

I have cited these two celebrated examples because, since they refer to the solution of the human drama, they are the most characteristic. But the syncopated method is applied throughout the novels, giving them a wonderful rapidity and total absence of delays. For example, at the end of *La Chartreuse*: "*Ici nous demandons la permission de passer, sans dire un seul mot, sur un espace de trois années.*"

This method of extreme abbreviation is also applied to the so-called minor works. Let's look at the end of *Vanina Vanini*: "*Vanina resta anéantie. Elle revint à Rome; et le journal annonce qu'elle vient d'épouser le prince Savelli.*"

It is a style which in its dryness may seem easy but which is in fact the fruit of an arduous quest and a continuous labour of elimination: a style which above all requires as foundation a vast store of ideas besides memory and experience, because any lack of substance would immediately become obvious. One might compare the style to those modern clock faces which show us the precise hour with total clarity although (or perhaps because) the figures are substituted by small lines...

When reading Stendhal's works (with proper attention of course and not to find out "what happens") – particularly the two major novels but to some extent all the others – one becomes aware that each of them is, shall we say, written in two columns consisting in equal measure of sensations described and transmitted normally and of a second series of sensations expressed only through a marked silence intended to attract the attention of the alert reader. To his lyrical and psychological observations Stendhal has from beginning to end applied the method unconsciously adopted by the greatest novelists and playwrights to express landscape and atmosphere: to suggest and evoke them with the faintest of touches, but almost never to describe. This method has the advantage first of all of permeating the narrative with the atmosphere (and in Stendhal's case the psychological observations), to make it always present rather than isolated in descriptive (or psychological) blocks dragged along by the flow of the story. And it has the further advantage of strengthening, through their rarity value, those purely descriptive passages which remain vividly in one's memory (for instance, the magnificent description of the Vosges in *Rouge et Noir*).

III

The Travel Writer

Rome, Naples et Florence is not only the first of Stendhal's works written after his unusual talents had reached maturity, but is also one of his most characteristic and significant. It is difficult to define, although perhaps one could suggest a subtitle: *Etudes sur les différents conceptions du bonheur à Milan, Bologne, Florence, Venise, Rome et Naples.* Further south Stendhal did not venture because, as he put it, "*au delà de Naples c'est l'Empire des Turcs; l'Italie est finie.*" With this work begins that series of travel books which form a special and notable part of the author's literary creativity.

It's now necessary to clarify the meaning of the expression "travel books" when referring to Stendhal. He did not at all mean to observe Italy and France in the way that Father Huc observed the customs of the Tibetans in that period. He intended merely to jot down the psychological impulses of the people, especially their attitudes "*au problème du bonheur qui est le problème de la vie*", and to see whether they corresponded to his own idea of happiness. It is this unity of purpose, this perfect homogeneity between his travel books and his great novels which gives the first category their high intellectual value. We must not deceive ourselves: *Les Promenades dans Rome*, the *Mémoires d'un touriste*, and this *Rome, Naples et Florence* are just one side of Stendhal's affectionate polemic with his times and with himself, the side not yet embodied in great fictitious canvases. . .

The most interesting part of these books is the myriad of apologues (they are called anecdotes but this is not quite the right word here) through which Stendhal illustrates his own views of life. The author attributes to himself incidents that befell others, assigns to others experiences that happened to him, and even invents stories which he claims to have extracted from newspapers (giving the title and the date) which had not had the opportunity (or the skill) to publish them. The taste for mystification and the disposition to cover one's traces (characteristic of the Carbonaro) have together helped to blend this conglomeration of anecdotes into a psychological unity without equal. On reading them one realises how impossible they would be to recount: such is the slenderness of their form, so numerous are the nuances of feeling conveyed in every line, that one would need to learn them by heart to be able to recount them without irreparable deformation.

It is said (and it's almost true) that Stendhal could not write short stories; certainly he was more at ease in the larger framework of the novel. Yet if the short story forced him to follow a pre-arranged plan (a novel can be "disordered", but a short story must be rigorously organised), nevertheless his talent for eliminating the unnecessary together with his lightning psychological insight allowed him to master – whether in ten lines or three pages – that narrative known as the anecdote in which composition is superfluous and the speed of intuition is everything.

In *Rome, Naples et Florence* we encounter for the first time in Stendhal's literary technique his ability almost to unite the three people who collaborate during the reading of a book: the author, the protagonist and the reader. The singular merit of his great masterpieces is partly derived from this perfect welding which we will discuss at length later on. For now it is enough to say that it is (like everything else worthwhile) the product of renunciation – for example, the elimination of any words which are too expressive or too sumptuous, words which might embellish a page but immediately place the reader outside the action, in the position of someone looking at a painting.

The work of a profound expert on the human heart – understood always as a variant of his own heart – and a highly sensitive observer of ambience, the labour of a writer whom disenchantment had already impelled towards ironic compassion, a work written with delightful celerity and a verve shorn of vulgarity, this book is the author's first great *réussite*, the first of his works as the perfect "improviser".

This last phrase is confirmed by the existence of a second version, revised and expanded, which contains many new anecdotes and observations and yet is like a fire which has lost its glare: it is the product of amendments to a text *already written* and is no longer the spontaneous expression of feelings long meditated in silence.

Promenades dans Rome is set later but it is so similar to *Rome, Naples et Florence* that if described separately I would be forced to repeat what I have tried to say about the earlier book. Yet one can see some minor differences. *Promenades dans Rome* is a guide for travellers, compiled with special attention to archaeology, written by a genius and brightened by a vaguely fictitious plot. The character sketches are delightful: Frédéric, the earnest and self-possessed man always in search of ruins and serious conversation; Paul, who prefers pretty young girls and tasty ice creams; and an anonymous lady who weeps while listening to love stories and goes mad about Cimarosa. Luckily there is no action. Readers can identify as they like with one or other of these characters, and the book seems to be written entirely by itself.

More conspicuous than in the previous volume is Stendhal's effusion of Epicurean wisdom. For him Italy, and Rome in particular, is the country which has contributed the most to mankind's greatest aspirations: "*l'attente du bonheur*". But it is precisely for this reason that "*il faut prendre garde à qui conseiller les voyages en Italie: les esprits grossiers qui préfèrent l'acte à l'attente en seront déçus.*"

Once again "*l'attente*"...

With *Promenades dans Rome* Stendhal reached the peak of his ability to interpret human character through travel; his later *Mémoires d'un touriste* are of similar but not greater quality. Together with some pages of Chateaubriand (conceived, however, in quite the opposite spirit), the *Promenades* are the greatest homage which has been paid to Rome, a city here understood as a living thing and not merely as a store of memories.

Now is the moment to point out yet again that astonishing lack of solidity in Italian literature from the fifteenth century to the end of the nineteenth. London was evoked by Fielding, Boswell and Dickens; the growth of Paris was followed step by step by Restif, Balzac, Stendhal, Flaubert and Zola; Pushkin could capture the gilded and ghostly charm of St Petersburg; Fontane secured the immortality of old Berlin which had disappeared long before that empire which fell to pieces under the weight of its own sins. But had it been depicted by Italians alone, Rome would have left no artistic trace between Boccaccio and D'Annunzio's *Il Piacere*. For a portrait we must resort to foreign eyes, and thank goodness they are good ones, the eyes of Du Bellay, Milton, Goethe, Chateaubriand, Stendhal and even Zola.

Le Rouge et le Noir

No exhortations to admire *Le Rouge et le Noir* are needed in 1955. The novel has transcended the human to attain the divine, and all people, believers or sceptics, will prostrate themselves before it. It strikes me as always relevant, however, to explain why the book should be admired...

Since it is pointless to catalogue Stendhal's brilliant gifts as poet, analyst of feelings and evoker of ambience, nothing is left for me except to try to show you the technical means which he used to express those gifts. In art the capacity to communicate is obviously everything, and in a novel we should be particularly interested by the methods used to communicate the passing of time, to make the narrative solid, to evoke the atmosphere and to handle the dialogue. These are, after all, things which offer the opportunity of being studied. It is like taking a clock to pieces. Observing in their correct sequence the springs, cogwheels, releases, screws and pivots, you will understand how it works. You will even be able to try to put it together again, and the clock will start to go if...if you have your own inner time by which to set the hands. This, however, is a condition which no-one can help you to fulfil. Either you have it or you haven't.

Let us look a little more closely at the little wheels of the mechanism. First of all there is the question of time, which is the first serious problem confronting the novelist and which can only be resolved by means of various devices. By occasionally slowing down the rhythm of the narrative, the reader must be given the impression that years have gone by during the couple of days spent reading the book. Undisputed master of the art of slowing-down was Tolstoy. *War and Peace* takes a week to read at most, but the feeling of ten years – the duration of the action – is clearly conveyed. The gradual estrangement of Anna and Vronsky fills about fifty pages of *Anna Karenina* and can be read in an hour. But the reader, unless he has been endowed with the hide of a rhinoceros, will have felt the slow passing of the months during which the affair declines.

How does one achieve this result? Certainly not by naively writing, "seven months went by during which... etc". That is the information of a railway timetable which reaches the brain but not the emotions. Instead it is necessary to suggest the same thing through imperceptible brush strokes that touch the pre-conscious. Read with attention those immortal chapters of *Anna Karenina*. You will see with what subtlety Tolstoy indicates that such and such an incident takes place in the dryness of summer ("she returned hot to the sitting-room and removed her straw hat"), another during the autumn rains ("Vronsky's boots left traces of mud on the paving"), and a third in the winter snows ("the cap hanging on the hat-stand had dripped sleet that was now melting"). In the fire of the first reading (and every first reading must be made without a pencil in hand, so that one can plunge into the furnace), these minute details will not even be noticed, as we will be captured by the romantic drama unfolding around us. But a sediment will remain in the pre-conscious. On closing the book you will not *know* but you will *feel* that several months have gone by.

Discreet and indirect information about the seasons is the most obvious method. But there are others which are more subtle: the use of the imperfect which gives a sense of unfilled continuity, details of physical changes, examples of recurrence and many other things. All done, thank goodness, in passing and almost concealed, because in this case the way of making one *remember* coincides with the way of *not making one notice*.

There is also, of course, the opposite method, that of acceleration, which is based on the same technique but in reverse. From the fusion of these two methods, the novelist (or the epic poet or the dramatist) appears as the master of time. And when the reader says that in *Anna Karenina* (or *L'Education sentimentale* or *I Malavoglia*), "everything is so lovely and seems so real", he is merely paying awkward homage to the skill with which the author has known how to express time, the "a priori" truth.

The modulation of the tempo is the chief (but not of course the only) quality of every great novelist or epic poet. Vital though insufficient by itself, it is the sun without which every other inventive faculty putrefies. The *Odyssey* lasts for ten years, *L'Education* effectively unfolds in thirty, in *Don Quixote* the evocation of time is delightful and extraordinary – a sultry sunset, eternal but not stationary – and in *L'Enlèvement de la Redoute*, the three seconds of real action seem like a very long period of grief and anger.

By contrast, one of the numerous defects of *Orlando Furioso* is Ariosto's complete ignorance of the question of time. One doesn't know if the action takes place over an afternoon or twenty years; or to be more precise, one knows only through explicit statements that reach the brain but do not move the emotions.

In *Rouge et Noir* the way of arranging time is one of the most brilliant in literature (although the method used in *La Chartreuse* is not inferior). There is none of the slowing down of *War and Peace* but rather a continuous acceleration. The duration of action actually described is less than the time taken to read it, so that the narration must be spurred on for it to unroll truly like the gallop of real horses. Stendhal had to sacrifice many things to the demands of time: we have lost some valuable and perhaps necessary pages of introspection. But everything is compensated for by the stupendous rhythm. The whole book flies straight and swift like an arrow. There is only one return to the past.

Another vital problem, the position of the narrator, is resolved in the best possible way. Elsewhere I have spoken of the scruples which worried earlier writers about the legitimacy of their omniscience of their characters' feelings. These scruples could be calmed by turning to the epistolary form which slowed down the action and made it easy to digress. Others preferred narration in the first person which allowed for deep investigation, albeit confined to the character who was telling the story... Still others, like Proust, narrated in the first person but supposed themselves to be blessed with the power of interpreting the thoughts of others. In this Proust was successful because he was a genius, but the method is bristling with dangers and absurdities.

Stendhal chooses the shortest and proudest way which might, for the sake of simplicity, be defined as God telling the story. Stendhal in divine garb knows the most hidden thoughts of every character, points them out to the reader who shares his all-seeingness, and leaves nothing in the shade except for what, in order to obtain heightened emotion, he does not wish to express.

At the beginning the novel is recounted in an indirect way, and the rude life of Verrières, the character of Monsieur de Rênal and the squalor of business matters going on all around him are seen through the mind of a witness who is not indifferent but outside the action. Yet when Julien arrives on the scene, the world is revealed as it appears to his eyes. Nevertheless, during the great row the centre and observatory of the universe is Monsieur de Rênal. And in her turn the simplicity of his wife is such that her thoughts are easily read by both her friend and her lover. In the second part, based in Paris, the world is seen in turn through Julien and Mathilde. Indeed in one scene we are transported successively in a few lines from the thoughts of one to those of the other in a dialogue which has no precursors (nor successors) in its total uncovering of two minds not by spoken words but by thoughts reported as if in footnotes...

The result of this almost incredibly acute technique... is the complete fusion of author, character and reader. The latter is no more an outsider observing the action but almost one of the actors in the drama himself.

Such an outcome is obtained mainly by means of "interior monologue". This way of doing things, which reached its acme with Proust, Joyce and Virginia Woolf, was employed by Stendhal in a more restrained manner as a means of revealing motives while not slowing down the action. This may look simple but it isn't. *Le Rouge et le Noir* is primarily a lyrical effusion and a novel of psychological analysis, but it is also a portrait of the time and a book in which events press upon each other. This last factor is certainly not a consideration in the works of the three authors mentioned a few lines above. But in Stendhal the demands of action produce an effort of concentration of the "interior monologues" which is not found in those writers for whom this means of expression became an end in itself. The action in *Ulysses*, for example, lasts for twenty-four hours and consists of a simple daily routine, but its reading requires at least five times as many days despite Joyce's magnificent efforts at concentration. But his are efforts of verbal concentration while Stendhal's are aimed at achieving a substantial concentration of psychological moments. From each of these he kept only the essential which he then subjected to the distillation of his own style, one of the sveltest that exists. The characters' "interior monologues" are extremely short – just a few lines. The transition between these and the rest of the story consists of some indirect sentences forming a gentle slope between one type of narrative and the other.

The reader is thus spared the mental wrenches suffered when switching from one letter to another in an epistolary novel or from a ten-page interior monologue to the direct action of a modern novel. He becomes aware of sudden changes of rhythm only during a second, intentionally careful reading. The fluidity of the narrative remains intact...

As for ambience, Stendhal does not provide the minute details needed to describe buildings and furniture with that film director's meticulousness sometimes used by Balzac to create grandiose poetic effects. Yet in most cases he does manage to evoke – I truly don't know how – the furniture and the buildings. When Julien penetrates Madame de Rênal's room after leaving the seminary, the sense of a close, shuttered place with stale, musty smells is rendered unmistakably, Heaven knows how. The heavy splendour of the La Môle mansion is portrayed in words, but there are only five of them ("*vastes salons, dorés et tristes*"). The settings of crucial incidents are not described at all but evoked by means of a simple, earlier, presentation. When the scene later unfolds, the reader can thus use the mental image formed before, sometimes long before, without having to subject himself to the double labour needed to picture the place in his mind and at the same moment pay attention to the development of one of the most complex scenes in the novel.

In short, the book's key scenes never occur in a place previously unknown. The church of Verrières, for example, where Julien's crime takes place, was shown to us at the beginning of the book with very light (and also rather macabre) nuances. The end of Chapter 8 of the first part prepares us for the scene which follows, that famous one in which Julien shakes Madame de Rênal's hand under the linden tree. The undescribed library of the La Môle mansion is first used for scenes of minor importance so that the reader is then forced to form a mental image of the place which will help provide the ambience for the storms unleashed by Julien and Mathilde on the same spot...

The ambience of a conflict, however, is only in small part composed of landscapes and buildings. It principally consists of people, institutions and customs. These elements, which are of much greater interest to Stendhal, are also drawn with greater explicitness, though always with outlines that are expressive but at the same time delicate and seldom emphasised. The narrow-mindedness of provincial society, the sense of permanent distrust in the seminary, the frivolity in fashionable circles and the sense of intrigue in others, are described like this in such a clear and memorable way that examples are superfluous.

The dialogue in *Rouge et Noir* is managed in a style so subtle as to pass unnoticed at first sight. The defect of so many novels (including some of the best!), which is to reveal people's inmost thoughts through what they say, has here disappeared. In real life verbal revelation is virtually absent. We understand much more of people's characters through their deeds, their glances, their stammering, the way they play with their fingers, their silences and their rapid way of talking, the colour of their cheeks, the speed of their stride – almost never through conversation which is always either a modest or a shameless mask disguising their inner feelings. Stendhal understood this perfectly: *his work contains no well-known passage of dialogue*. The principal characters are those whose words are least reported. When Julien refuses to marry Elisa, we are given only a summary of what he answered; when he asks Monsieur de la Môle permission to go away in order to escape the consequences of his love, we know only the words of the old gentleman's reply. Wherever he can, Stendhal tries to avoid direct conversation. He prefers to report, by all manner of allusive comment, by rectifying what has been said, which this method allows a writer as shrewd as he is. . .

This too lengthy exposition of some technical aspects of *Rouge et Noir* has certainly been boring and may also seem superfluous. But I don't think it unnecessary, firstly because in art the "technique of execution" is everything, the artist being nothing more than a fellow who can express himself. Secondly, because . . . much of what I have written here applies to the other works, especially *La Chartreuse*. And thirdly because the potency of Stendhal's technique has been the cause of many of the negative moral judgments pronounced on this novel.

At the time of publication there was much indignation at the author's moral indifference. Fifty years later, when Stendhal's reputation began to "rocket" towards its present glory, many continued to be scandalised by its apologia for unscrupulous *arrivisme* and by the lack of "heart" which they managed to discern in that "monster" Julien Sorel. A short time ago I heard it said that in *Rouge et Noir* one can perceive the devil's tail.

It is perhaps because I am accustomed to the sight of that reprehensible tail, which I see squirming slyly in every corner of my field of vision, but the fact is that I have never felt greatly scandalised when reading *Rouge et Noir*. Julien Sorel has always seemed to me a young man who was too ambitious, it's true, too lacking in scruples, too inclined to run for shelter under the petticoats of his mistresses; but nothing worse than what we can see in numerous acquaintances. Compared to Dorian Gray and

Lafcadio and Morel and even the Reverend Slope, he is even a little angel. I can discern "sin" but not an exceptional evil. He is a common type, the only unusual thing about him being the fact that he is an example of energy in a burnt-out generation. I will say more. I perceive in him something pathetic and in his creator the inclination to blame his wrongdoings on that particular period of history.

It is undeniable, however, that the impression of Julien's deep amorality is too widespread for it to be completely erroneous. Yet in my view this is a misunderstanding that springs precisely from such a singularly perfect technique.

There are thousands of rascals like Julien in real life and dozens in art. But he is one of the very few to have been described with a technique that floodlights his entire (though rather banal) iniquity. A flea enlarged ten times under a microscope seems an apocalyptic monster... yet the flea itself remains the same relatively innocuous insect. In the novel we are not dealing with a monster but with a character monstrously alive, much more alive than those people of flesh and bone whom we meet every day and whose hands we shake without fellow-feeling but also without horror. Stendhal's technique has succeeded in stripping naked for the reader that same Julien who appears to the other characters still clad with considerable merits and with some virtues. And all nakedness, unless sculpted by Praxiteles, is repulsive. Yet without it one cannot study anatomy.

One other comment still directed against *Rouge et Noir* is more serious because it is an artistic criticism. Many readers – and not third-rate ones either – remain bewildered by Julien's end, which they find psychologically unjustified, technically slovenly and aesthetically bankrupt. To me this view is incomprehensible.

The crisis of the book, from the arrival of Madame de Rênal's letter onwards, seems to me the inevitable consequence of the character and behaviour of Julien. What else could it have been? The book's ending strikes me as its greatest merit, and I have already tried to explain why. In it we find not only the logical way out of the situation but also the likeable sincerity of Stendhal who has no further interest in Julien from the moment that the latter has *found*. The author has hurriedly killed off his character in order to free himself from him. An ending of charming tragic quality without equal. That Stendhal did not bother to explain his reasons must be attributed, I think, to a double cause: firstly he was writing avowedly for "the happy few" gifted with insight and not for those who need explanations; and secondly he did not explain because the ending was justified by the fact that it was *real*. Berthet had committed his own crime for the same reasons and in the same conditions as Julien. What is there to explain?

The fifty pages following Julien's crime are very peculiar. The world is no longer seen through Julien but through an indifferent and colourless X. How indeed could Julien see if for the author he was already dead? The body alone was still living, to be disturbed by the *mauvaus air* of the prison.

So dead was Julien that it is not even stated that he was executed. His last moments are mentioned and so is his corpse, but there is nothing about his death. Here we have one of the most characteristic moments of Stendhal's "elisions". Let us read it. On his last day Julien says to his friend Fouqué, "'*Ces bons congréganistes de Besançon font argent de tout; si tu sais t'y prendre, ils te vendront ma dépouille mortelle.' Fouqué réussit dans sa triste négociation. Il passait la nuit seul dans sa chambre, auprès du corps de son ami, lorsqu'à sa grande surprise. . .*"etc

The impetuous, handsome and dynamic Julien utters his last words to teach a friend how to ransom his corpse.

It is futile to explain the pathos of this situation to anyone who lacks the sensibility to perceive it for himself.

La Chartreuse de Parme

As is well-known, *La Chartreuse* is the modern transposition of the story of Vannozza Farnese. The story has everything which we will find in the novel; the aunt's love for her prelate nephew, the prison, the escape, the attempted poisoning. Everything in short except the Charterhouse.

This renowned novel, perhaps the greatest, certainly the most lovable that has ever been written, is clearly divided into two parts, of equal value but different tone. The first introduces us to a Fabrizio who is ambitious, restless and not very scrupulous – a rich brother of Julien. And except for the miraculous first thirty pages, the atmosphere is much the same as that in which Sorel struggled. The first part is a work of the highest class, but it is also a work with a precursor.

The second part (which in my opinion begins immediately after Giletti's death) owes nothing to anything.

Here I want to put you on your guard against what I am about to say. What you will hear is my purely subjective impression, an impression that might be called colourful or musical, but one which will not be in accord with anybody else's reading and which even finds some contradictions in my own. To cite an example dear to yourselves, you will recall the *William Tell* overture which is enjoyed by some unqualified listeners as representing a thunderstorm followed by sunshine, by a second group as a horse-race and by another section of the public as an idyll interrupted by an explosion of wrath as the people see their idyll threatened, but later on recovered. And although it is in fact none of these things, you will not succeed in dampening the convictions of these uneducated spectators because their views come not from the intellect but from emotional sources.

At this point I must say that, while being aware that the story of *La Chartreuse* is packed with horrible plots, incessant fears, sinister characters (the Duke, Rassi and possibly Count Mosca) and the cruellest prisons – while knowing these things and knowing too that they are not merely symbolic but taken from an appalling, documentable reality, yet – I repeat – although my brain is aware of these things, when I read *La Chartreuse* I forget them completely and am smitten by an incomparable peacefulness that brings me serenity and calm.

I love comparisons and want to dish one out that will fortunately take us far from the vulgar swamps of opera. All of us know and love Dante's *Purgatorio*. How many of us, however, have reflected that it represents a place of punishment, that souls suffer torments there comparable to those in Hell? Every reader, I believe and hope, reaches the last canto with the impression of having crossed a region of tranquil serenity, permanently illuminated by a benign sun. It is not like that, as one can see from the list of torments at hand. But it becomes like that, for the majority of readers, by virtue of Dante's art.

I know very well that Ernest IV is a foul character, based on the figures of Francis of Modena, Francis II of Austria and the young Charles Albert. I know that Earth (and Hell) is full of people like Rassi and that the citadel of Parma is a place of torment worthy of Piranesi... I realise that Count Mosca is a perfect portrait of those ministers and underlings, completely egotistical and unscrupulous, who are smaller and nastier copies of their great model Metternich; I am aware of how many betrayals, poisoned pills and knife stabs are woven into the plot of the novel. I will say more. I know very well that Stendhal wished to arouse the reader's indignation against such men and such methods.

I know all this but I repeat that it makes no difference to me. As far as I am concerned, Stendhal's aim has missed. He wanted to depict the Inferno but instead has created the most adorable Dantesque Purgatory.

La Chartreuse overflows with tragedies, but to me they appear like submerged rocks beneath strong but calm waters which they do not disturb. For me this is the triumph of "ataraxy". The novel's characters move in a divine calm, graceful swans who navigate the waters of Lethe without danger.

The only disturbers of the scene are Ferrante Palla and General Fabio Conti, characters who are almost humorous. When the great reservoir of water is opened, I seem to hear the graceful sound of those delightful meandering waterfalls which enhance the silence of the Villa d'Este. Fabrizio's giddy escape merely arouses admiration for his acrobatic and dancing skills; he appears to me as a sort of Nijinsky, a creator of beautiful postures. The tribulations, regrets and plots of La Sanseverina are entirely blotted out by her maternal beauty and the sweetest of smiles. And Count Mosca is an adorable gentleman, selfless and witty. For me the greatest triumph of the art of Stendhal, that devotee of overpowering passion, is his achievement in completing his work with a masterpiece in which passion is hidden and over which, instead of the pitiless midday son of *Vanina Vanini* and *Rouge et Noir*, there shines "*la douceur étrange de cet après-midi qui n'a jamais de fin*".

Is it really possible that this impression could be mine alone? I know too few people who have read the book except as a thriller to be able to check the uniqueness of my view. And even accepting that it is unique or extremely rare, is it derived from incipient schizophrenia or from a perhaps arbitrary interpretation of certain elements found in *La Chartreuse*?

As Mallarmé's faun would say, "*Réfléchissons*."

Or rather let us carefully read a random passage, for example the end of Chapter 13 in Part One. Let's begin with the paragraph which starts with "*Il rentra chez lui haletant de fureur*". From that moment a succession of terrible events unfolds. First of all there are the spies on almost every line. Then Count M throws himself on Fausta, or rather "*il prit son poignard et se précipita sur elle*". Afterwards comes the incident with Bettina disguised as a man, and after that Fabrizio wounds an individual who assaults him.

Then there is the big scene during which Fabrizio is attacked while escaping from the sedan chair: "*Tue! tue tout ce qui porte des torches*"; on the morrow there is "*beaucoup de sang répandu sur le pavé*". There follows the (for us) comic interlude of the learned man with red hair who spends a month in prison; and it all ends with a duelling scene witnessed by a clamorous gathering of peasants. Not even in ten pages of *Les Mystères de Paris* is there so much violence. And yet I feel neither fear nor disgust, but rather a calm descending over me "*qui tient plus du ciel que de l'enfer*". Why? Because a light irony is sprinkled over everything, beginning with that "*haletant de fureur*". Then there is Fabrizio "*qui se faisait ainsi la morale*". Bettina in disguise is described "*comme un être microscopique*". Immediately afterwards it is reported that "*elle était fort jolie ce qui enleva Fabrice à ses idées morales*". As soon as one of the *bravi* is wounded by Fabrizio, "*il lui dit du ton le plus respectueux: 'Votre Altesse me fera une bonne pension pour cette blessure'*". After the fighting around the sedan chair, which is also recounted "*sur le ton badin*", "*la duchesse rit beaucoup*". The whole episode of the arrest of the "*savant homme*" is dealt with in a humorous tone ("*porter de petits pistolets est un grand crime*"). And the duel as well is treated with a tone of "*plaisanterie*" ("*C'est tout simplement un duel à mort*"). The result of this accumulation of soft words (and I have not transcribed all of them) describing violent events is that the narrative proceeds with a graceful gait.

And I can swear that the episode was chosen by randomly opening the book.

On opening *La Chartreuse* wherever you like, you will easily be able to check that this is the tone Stendhal always adopts when he narrates violent events – at least when he narrates them, because often he leaves them to be guessed. Why does he do this in a novel which is meant to be tragic and "accusing"? For a very simple reason: the events are not meant to be recounted as they *are* but as they *appear* to the frivolous, though at the same time courageous and arrogant, temperament of Fabrizio, the temperament of a "society man" who reduces the external world to his own level. Keep this axiom in mind and the reading of *La Chartreuse* will bring you fresh, more delightful and I believe more authentic intellectual joys.

Perhaps I am not schizophrenic.

This method of narration is prodigiously difficult: the author must remain the whole time inside the skin of his protagonist. And since the world is seen entirely through the latter's eyes, the reader will also view it through that mind which is disenchanted, agreeable, easy-going, gentlemanly and not very intelligent.

The result is that the reader runs through the thirty years which the novel encompasses with the feelings of pure amusement, detachment and insubstantiality that such a writer can transmit to those of similar temperament. One is dragged to the supreme pleasure of lightness and spectacle which is what the world was for Fabrizio del Dongo.

How many Fabrizios I have known! People for whom Fascist authorities, grim prefects, prison warders and avowed trollops were seen only through their most superficial and often pleasant sides, not through lack of penetration but through superficiality and a childish trust in life. Through such eyes the world is populated by "fine fellows" and "good girls" and, if these excellent companions do something really terrible, it is easy to excuse them by not speaking of it, or rather by trying to efface the memory of their behaviour for fear that the harmonious world they had built would crumble into pieces.

(This has nothing to do with indulgence.)

It is through one of these types that the dirty and tragic world of *La Chartreuse* is revealed to us; and the peace which reigns in these singular minds is transmitted to the reader. In short, *"omnia laevia laeviis"*. Through a mind which possesses no sense of tragedy, everything appears as comedy.

The wonder worked by Stendhal consists in having transferred his readers of 1839 (and of 1955) into the mind of a genial young nobleman of the beginning of the nineteenth century who is nonchalant, voluptuous and mildly sentimental, and making them understand the Great Fear of the Counter-Revolution as Fabrizio himself was able to understand it.

The technical means used to obtain this effect are the usual ones already listed: the devices for achieving an impression of time are inverted so as to give that sense of gentle flowing and amusing tedium which the subject radiates.

In certain works one has a strong desire to dismantle the mechanisms of the genius's clock: an irrational "something" is always left.

This observation allows me to avoid a close examination of *La Chartreuse*. I will point out only some episodes.

First of all the famous description of the Battle of Waterloo. This is universally admired, contrasted with Hugo's celebrated account of the same battle and compared in effectiveness to conflicts described by Tolstoy.

This Stendhalien Waterloo is indeed admirable, but there are no comparisons to be made. Hugo's battle is the struggle as it is seen. . . by a poet who aspired to be a successful prophet. Tolstoy's terribly muddled combats are the ingenious memories of an authentic combatant. But Stendhal's Waterloo is a battle as it is seen just by Fabrizio, whose happily superficial nature prevents him from understanding grave matters or even from perceiving danger except with difficulty. Falling shells are for him merely annoying contraptions which spatter a good deal of mud that might dirty his clothes. Having left the "nursery" of Grianta only two weeks before, he can only see the "nuisances", never the dangers. In fact it is really in these pages that Fabrizio's delightful sorcery begins to work upon the reader.

The chapters on Fabrizio's prison (actually his two prisons) seem to me among the finest in *La Chartreuse*, not so much for their artistic merit as for their intellectual and lyrical importance. In no other section has Stendhal's "double-column" system been so happily employed. While the one side reveals the usual soothing amusement of the prisoner's mentality which trans-mutes the horrors into a game for himself and tranquil delight for the reader, one notices the underlying lyricism of the author who has taken his well-loved double from the ordinary world, and on a third plane one catches a glimpse of that same desire possessed by

Goethe in the *Wahlverwandtschaften* of creating a distant and artificial world in which to move his favourites around.

From this shrewdest of counterpoints, from the fusion and occasional opposition of these three themes are born what are perhaps the most poetic pages of French prose.

Having said this, I fear I have not sufficiently stressed both how the worldly optimistic vision bestows its tone on the whole book and bequeathes its consoling lightness, and also how the author's own harsher *Weltanschauung* can frequently be seen as well. It is due to this constant alternation of themes that *La Chartreuse* is at the same time so homogeneous and so varied.

A final word on the last pages of the book. From the moment we hear Clélia's voice in the night say "*Entre ici, ami de mon coeur*" ("*et plus tard un ange entr'ouvrant les portes*") we enter a poetic Elysium in which melancholy is transmuted into joy without losing any of its restraint or modesty, while the frequent ironic phrases remove any possible tastelessness. And finally appears the Charterhouse which has given its name to the work, and which has not hitherto been mentioned. It emerges suddenly like a tomb, like a haven of tranquil joy. In *La Chartreuse* people don't really die, they just withdraw by imperceptible steps towards incorporeal memory.

Never has such high and graceful poetry been expressed in such banal language. *La Chartreuse* is the purest miracle of feeling and style.

"To the happy few"